Researching the Law

Copyright Acknowledgments

Researching the Law

David Bachman, Steve Donweber, Ellen Minot
Richardson, Jennifer Robble, Stefanie Weigmann

Edited by Steve Donweber

A Shepard's Adhesive Annotation from 1906.

Table of Contents

Introduction

Legal research is the process by which lawyers, students, professors and judges investigate the law to determine its dimensions and requirements. Effective legal research will or can show whether certain acts are criminal, certain conduct is tortious, a contract has been breached, a particular rule of practice or evidence has been violated, and generally, whether any given action or activity is lawful or unlawful.

Legal research is therefore vital to the study and practice of law. Indeed, legal research is almost always the first step taken in the representation of a client and/or the resolution of a legal issue.

Successful legal research requires knowledge of where to "find" the "law." This is not an abstract inquiry. Although some discussions of the "location" or "sources" of law involve a wide-ranging inquiry into "[c]ustom, tradition, principles of morality, and economic, political, philosophical, and religious thought,"[1] this one won't. Rather, for the purpose of this book, a "source" of law is a very practical and tangible thing; it is, quite simply, the place where the law is published. Put another way, it's the place where lawyers and students "find" the law as it is written down.[2]

With that definition in mind, sources of law—the places where the law is written down—fall generally into two major categories, **primary sources** and **secondary sources**. A **primary source** for law is the law itself, i.e., the collection of words that constitute the rules, customs, and practices of a community. Put another way, primary authority is the actual constitution, statute, case, or regulation that is produced by the legislature, the court, or an executive agency. Obviously, locating applicable primary authority is one of the key goals of legal research.

---

[1]   STEVEN M. BARKAN ET AL., FUNDAMENTALS OF LEGAL RESEARCH 1 (9th ed. 2009).

[2]   Black's Law Dictionary defines "law" as:

The aggregate of legislation, judicial precedents, and accepted legal principles; the body of authoritative grounds of judicial and administrative action; esp., the body of rules, standards, and principles that the courts of a particular jurisdiction apply in deciding controversies brought before them <the law of the land>.

BLACK'S LAW DICTIONARY 962 (9th ed. 2009).

By way of contrast, a **secondary source** is a source that is "about" the law—not the law itself, but a discussion of the law that may include citations to primary authority, explanations, interpretations, and the like. Examples of secondary sources include law review articles, legal encyclopedias, treatises, horn books, and practice guides. Secondary sources are extraordinarily valuable as they can provide an overview of a particular area of law that includes explanations, citations to primary authority, important exceptions to legal rules, and other content that the researcher would otherwise have to find and piece together separately. For this reason, we recommend that most legal research begin in a secondary source.

This book will mirror the research classes for 1L's at Boston University School of Law and, thus, will discuss researching primary sources, like cases and statutes; and secondary sources, like legal encyclopedias, American Law Reports, and practice guides, in detail. The book will also discuss updating your research, which means ensuring that the primary sources to which you cite are still valid for the legal proposition you are discussing or upon which you are relying. We conclude the research and updating chapters with practice questions, a couple pages for taking notes, and the answer key for the questions.

Finally, as an alternative to researching in expensive databases, we will identify some no-cost and low-cost ways to conduct legal research. This will include a brief look at quality websites, less expensive databases, and efficient methods.

Good luck in your research!

*   *   *

Many thanks to Lauren Stoia for her skillful research and drafting with regard to the section on Alternatives to High-Cost Databases.

The United States Legal System

The United States Constitution established three branches of government: the legislature, the judiciary, and the executive. Each of the 50 states has a more-or-less parallel system. Primary legal authority flows from all three branches.

The legislature—whether federal or state—produces **statutes**, which are laws passed by a legislative body following introduction of a bill, a complex deliberative process, and interaction between and among both houses of the legislature and the executive branch.[3] Statutes often, but not always, frame their requirements in general language that is subject to interpretation by courts or amplification by executive agencies.

The judiciary, i.e. our system of courts, produces **case law**. Case law is comprised of written opinions by judges resolving all or part of a dispute between two or more parties in the course of a civil or criminal proceeding. Case law will often interpret the common law[4] or a statute in the context of an individual dispute. The interpretation creates precedent, which will then shape future interpretations of the common law or the applicable statute in other disputes.

The executive branch, or more precisely executive agencies, promulgate[5] **regulations**. In one sense, regulations provide the details for the broad policy mandates set forth in statutes. Put another way, regulations are the rules an agency writes to explain how a statute will be implemented. In some cases the rules relate to a specific statute and in other cases to the statute establishing an agency. These rules have the legal force of the statute behind them. Rules too are often interpreted by case law.

---

[3]   Sounds easy, right?

[4]   Common law, for the most part, is based solely on other judicial decisions and does not involve interpretation of statutes or regulations.

[5]   The process by which executive agencies "carry out . . . formal . . . rulemaking by publishing the proposed regulation, inviting public comments, and approving or rejecting the proposal." BLACK'S LAW DICTIONARY 1334 (9th ed. 2009).

The official organization chart of the United States Government is below.

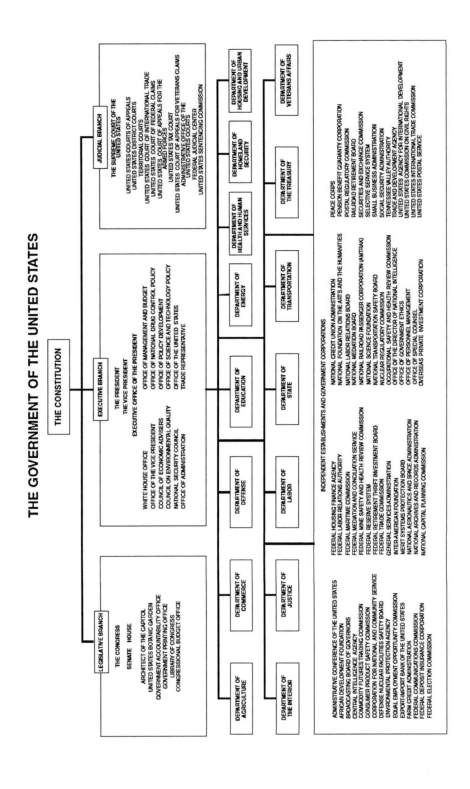

<u>Citations</u>

Legal citation is the method by which we refer to the sources of law, whether primary or secondary, that we rely upon when drafting court documents or legal memoranda, law school assignments, law review articles, and judicial opinions.

Citations are shorthand notations that permit the identification and location of a particular source. Thus, elements of a citation generally include what the source is, where it can be found, the year it was created or went into effect, and for all primary sources and some secondary, the relevant jurisdiction.

Mastering legal citation means mastering the profession-wide standards for citation set forth in *The Bluebook: A Uniform System of Citation*, published by the Columbia, Harvard, and University of Pennsylvania Law Reviews, and the Yale Law Journal.

Examples of citation format are contained within the discussions regarding specific sources.

*   *   *

Legal Research Method

Legal research is a process. It is a process that involves the distillation of key concepts involved in any particular legal problem, the selection of the proper source in which to research those concepts, and then an analysis of your research results.

The same four steps are used in legal research whether researching online or in print.

1.   Analyze problem and formulate key terms or concepts.

Legal issues almost always begin with a story, generally one told you by a client or supervisor. The story outlines a problem or challenge. Perhaps your client is being sued in New York in a shareholder derivative action for allegedly improper payments to interested directors. Or, perhaps your supervisor would like to see an analysis of the law related to dog bites in the state of Iowa.

It doesn't really matter what the story is because your approach to it will always be the same. The first step is to analyze the story told you and distill its key concepts and terms. This is generally the **who, what, where, when, and why** of the story.

Who?

In addition to determining which person is likely to be the plaintiff or the defendant, you want to be on the lookout for special relationships between the parties. Common relationships include parent/child, doctor/patient, attorney/client, landlord/tenant, and employer/employee. You may also be interested in fiduciaries, invitees, executors, and others to whom the law assigns special roles.

What?

Every factual scenario is a story composed of plot points. Your job is to determine which facts in the story are legally significant. You also want to think of legal keywords relating to the plot points and determine potential claims or defenses based on the plot points.

Where?

The location where the incident took place may be relevant for a couple of reasons. First, the geographic location of the incident may determine which state's law applies and which court has jurisdiction. Additionally, location may be a legally relevant fact. For example, in instances of landlord liability for injuries to tenants' guests, the outcome might differ if the injury took place in the common area of an apartment building as opposed to a tenant's unit.

When?

The date of the incident is important for statute of limitations purposes, but should also be considered when determining what the law was at the time the incident occurred. For example, if your client had a campfire in his backyard on May 31st, and the state he lived in passed a statute criminalizing this behavior on the following July 1st, the dates would be very relevant if the state attempted to prosecute your client under the statute for the fire he lit before the statute's effective date. The "when" question also includes the order in which particular events occurred. The sequence of events and the amount of time in between them are often crucial when one is trying to prove causation.

Why?

You are not always going to be able to answer the "why" question, but it can be relevant. In criminal law, offenses are often distinguished based on the intent, or mens rea, that accompanies the act. Similarly, in contracts, the outcome may differ depending on whether a party acted in good faith.

We can apply these ideas to the two simple examples noted earlier. In the case of your client sued in New York, the key concepts/terms are "New York," "shareholder derivative action," "payments," and "interested directors." In the case of the supervisor interested in Iowa law, the key concept/terms are "Iowa" and "dog bites." We will use these terms when we research applicable law.

2. **Select a jurisdiction when searching for primary authority; know your jurisdiction when searching for secondary.**

Legal authority is jurisdiction specific, whether the jurisdiction is federal or that of an individual state. Researching in the proper jurisdiction is therefore vital. In our examples, the jurisdictions are New York and Iowa.

3. **Use key terms to search an index or a database.**

This step is where the action is. Here, take your key terms and enter them into the search box in an appropriate online database or look them up in the index to an appropriate print source. This will provide you with a set of potentially relevant results for analysis.

4. **Analyze results.**

The final step is to analyze your set of potentially relevant results and determine which among them is applicable to your legal issue. If your research has been effective, you should be able to answer the question your client or supervisor has asked. Often your results will point you to more sources, which will require more analysis. This step is therefore iterative because you improve and hone your results as you learn more about the relevant area of law.

*   *   *

We will apply the legal research method to finding secondary sources, cases, and statutes in the chapters that follow.

*   *   *

Searching in Legal Databases

Generally

The major legal databases used in law school and practice are Westlaw and LexisNexis. There are also a number of minor and newer databases. These include Fastcase, Loislaw, Casemaker, and Bloomberg Law.[6] For our purposes, their content is the same.

All databases contain the main sources of American primary legal authority: statutes, cases, and regulations. The larger databases also contain extensive secondary source holdings, including law review articles, treatises, practice guides, legal encyclopedias, and hornbooks.

We are going to focus mostly on Westlaw and Lexis, but the process of searching is generally the same for most legal databases. Westlaw and Lexis have recently implemented new platforms called WestlawNext and Lexis Advance. The new platforms change the research experience considerably, but still provide essentially the same functionality. In any case, the four-step research method remains the same.

* * *

Using WestlawNext and Lexis Advance

The WestlawNext and Lexis Advance search engines operate in fundamentally the same way.

Searching

Both Westlaw and LexisNexis allow for **natural language** searching and **terms and connectors** searching.

Natural Language Searching

A **natural language** search is very much like a "Google" search. It is based on an algorithm that determines which results are relevant to your query

---

[6] Bloomberg Law has emerged in recent years as a competitor to Westlaw and LexisNexis. While an excellent resource for legal research in general, Bloomberg Law is particularly good for researching dockets, court documents, and business and financial information.

(and your results are then ranked by relevance). An example of such an algorithm is one that determines relevance based on how frequent your search terms appear and how close the terms are to each other. A natural language search does not require any special symbols or connectors between terms. Just enter your terms in the appropriate database search box and click "search." With a natural language search, the terms you use do not need to have identical matches in the documents retrieved (as they do in a terms and connectors search).

Terms & Connectors Searching

A **terms and connectors** or Boolean search does not use a search algorithm the way a natural language search does. Rather, the terms and connectors search requires the user to identify the specific terms she wants to see in every document that the search engine returns and, *very importantly,* the user also specifies the relationships between her chosen terms. This requires the use of **connectors** and other special symbols between terms. **For example:**

> **("brown fox" /2 quick) /s "lazy dog"**

If you use this query, you are telling the search engine to retrieve every document in the database in which the phrase **brown fox** appears *within 2 words* of the word **quick** and in which **brown fox** and **quick** appear in the *same sentence* as **lazy dog.** The search engine will only retrieve those documents that meet your criteria exactly, and for that reason, a terms and connectors search can be very useful if precision is required.

If no documents meet your criteria in a terms and connectors search, you will **get zero** results. You will not get zero results using a natural language search as the search engine will generally always provide at least some results relevant to your query.

Searching is an effective way to research legal resources of all types. However, there are circumstances where use of an index, table of contents, or the West Digest System (for cases) can yield better results. We will discuss these different research methods and the appropriate circumstances in which to use them within.

*　　*　　*

Researching Secondary Sources

Researching Secondary Sources

What is a Secondary Source?

As noted in the introductory material, a **secondary source** is a source that is "about" the law—not the law itself, but a discussion of the law that often includes citations to primary authority, explanations, interpretations, and legal commentary. In this chapter, we will examine different types of secondary sources including legal dictionaries, legal encyclopedias, American Law Reports, horn books, treatises, law journals, and practice guides.

*　　*　　*

Start Your Research with Secondary Sources

We recommend starting your research in an appropriate secondary source for two main reasons: (1) secondary sources provide general overviews and explanations of areas of law, and (2) secondary sources provide citations to primary authority; in other words, to the law itself.

*　　*　　*

General Overview of Area of Law

Secondary sources are a great place to start your research when you don't know a lot about the area of law implicated by your factual scenario. Secondary sources provide detailed explanations of the law in accessible language, and the explanations, in turn, provide context and background for the applicable primary authority. This contextual knowledge enhances understanding of the entire area of law as opposed to isolated pieces of it.

*　　*　　*

Citations to Primary Authority

You usually will not cite to secondary sources in documents filed with a court as they are not considered authoritative, so the second reason to start your research with secondary sources is to obtain citations to primary authority. Secondary sources are usually written by experts in the field, so you can count on them to provide citations to the major cases and statutes necessary to understand the law in a particular area.

* * *

Which Secondary Sources to Use?

When you start your first legal job you will be confronted with a number of different kinds of assignments. As we mentioned, secondary sources can help you accomplish these assignments in the most efficient way possible.

* * *

Massachusetts Practice

For example, suppose you were asked to prepare a defense for a Massachusetts resident who has been charged with Driving Under the Influence. Your first step would not be to look at a statute. Or even to look at caselaw. Rather you would look to a terrific secondary source called **Massachusetts Practice**.

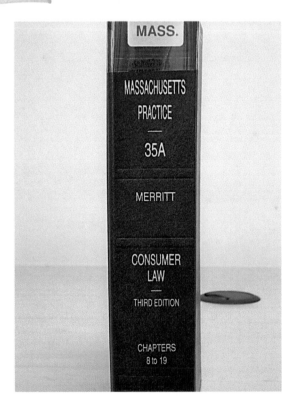

Practice guides like Massachusetts Practice provide jurisdiction-specific "how to's" with regard to both litigation and transactional law. Practice guides are often the best secondary source to use when practicing law in a particular jurisdiction.

In our case, you would see that Massachusetts Practice has an entire volume devoted to Drunk Driving Defense written by an attorney who has practiced many years in this area.

MASSACHUSETTS
PRACTICE SERIES™
Volume 50
_____

Drunk Driving Defense

From the summary of the contents of this volume shown below, you can see how valuable this resource is; it covers the entire range of issues facing a lawyer when defending against a drunk driving charge. Without this volume, a lawyer would have to assemble all of this material herself, without the benefit of anyone else's expertise.

Summary of Contents

Chapter 1. Offenses
Chapter 2. The Stop
Chapter 3. The Encounter
Chapter 4. Arrest and Booking
Chapter 5. The Chemical Test
Chapter 6. Citation Issues
Chapter 7. Release on Bail
Chapter 8. Drivers License Implications
Chapter 9. Client Interview/Investigation
Chapter 10. Pretrial Conference/Pretrial Motions/Pleas
Chapter 11. The Trial
Chapter 12. Acquittal, Dismissal and Sentencing
Chapter 13. Post-Conviction Relief

In general, Massachusetts Practice provides an overview of many areas of state substantive law in addition to civil and criminal procedure. Massachusetts Practice is an extremely useful resource for Massachusetts lawyers because it focuses solely on the law of Massachusetts. Massachusetts Practice is available in print as well as online through WestlawNext.

*   *   *

Legal Encyclopedias

Another assignment that new attorneys commonly get is to do a survey of the law over multiple jurisdictions. Suppose you are working on a team that is trying to make a unique legal argument in your jurisdiction regarding the requirement of paying college tuition as part of child support. You have been assigned to see how other jurisdictions treat the issue. Do you turn to Massachusetts Practice? No, because Massachusetts Practice only tells you the law in Massachusetts. A better source for this question is a **legal encyclopedia**.

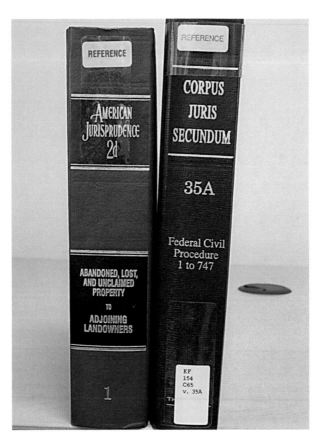

A legal encyclopedia is a multi-volume resource containing (in alphabetical order) general discussions on areas of and topics regarding law. Unlike a practice guide, it is not a "how to" resource, but rather one designed to provide general and background information only.

National Legal Encyclopedias

There are two major encyclopedias that are national in scope: *Corpus Juris Secundum* (CJS) and *American Jurisprudence 2d* (Am. Jur. 2d). These encyclopedias discuss areas governed by both federal and state law, and contain citations to statutes and cases from all fifty states in addition to the relevant federal laws. *Corpus Juris Secundum* is available on WestlawNext and in print. *American Jurisprudence 2d* is available on both WestlawNext and Lexis Advance. The library also has Am. Jur. 2d in print.

State Legal Encyclopedias

Many states have their own legal encyclopedias as well. These, for the most part, are available on WestlawNext in the Secondary Sources category for each state. Like the national encyclopedias, state encyclopedias have indexes and can be searched by keyword online.

A solution to our legal research question was contained in American Jurisprudence 2d, as you can see below.

§ 954   College expenses—Relevant factors

Research References
West's Key Number Digest, Child Support ☞115, 116, 119, 120

In determining a parent's contribution to a child's college expenses, the factors to be considered include: whether the parent, if still living with the child, would have contributed toward the costs of the requested education;[1] the effect of the background, values, and goals of the parent on the reasonableness of the child's expectation of a higher education;[2] and the relationship of the requested education to any prior training and to the overall long-range goals of the child.[3] In addition, it is proper to consider the amount of the contribution sought,[4] the ability of the parent to pay that cost,[5] and the relative financial resources of both parents.[6] Also to be considered are the

*   *   *

Another source that can help you finish your assignment regarding paying college tuition as part of child support is **American Law Reports** or **ALR**.

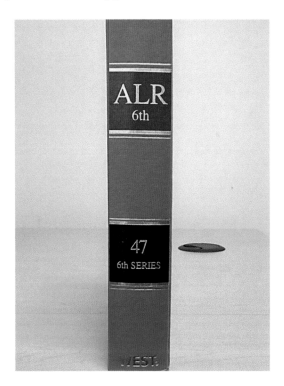

The American Law Reports is a secondary source that is broken into six (and counting) chronologically ordered series, as well as a separate series focusing solely on federal law. ALR includes articles called **annotations**, which are reprints of cases or detailed discussions on narrow issues of law. The annotations collect citations to cases from across jurisdictions that illustrate various approaches to the legal issue at hand.

ALR and legal encyclopedias can help you track down the treatment of this relatively narrow area of law, paying tuition as part of child support, across multiple jurisdictions. As you can see from the scan below from 99 A.L.R.3d 322, there is an annotation directly on point. Finding it took maybe five minutes using the ALR print index.

RESPONSIBILITY OF NONCUSTODIAL DIVORCED PARENT TO PAY FOR, OR CONTRIBUTE TO, COSTS OF CHILD'S COLLEGE EDUCATION

---

*   *   *

Federal Practice and Procedure

It seems that your practice and expertise are growing, and now you have a case in federal court. Good for you! During the course of the case, a question arises as to the proper method of serving process under Federal Rule of Civil Procedure 4. Don't fret! Luckily, there is a multi-volume resource that will allow you to find all the cases which have interpreted this particular rule of civil procedure, and the resource is called **Federal Practice and Procedure**.

FEDERAL PRACTICE
AND
PROCEDURE®

By

The Late CHARLES ALAN WRIGHT
Charles Alan Wright Chair in Federal Courts
The University of Texas

ARTHUR R. MILLER
Bruce Bromley Professor of Law, Harvard University

Federal Practice and Procedure, also referred to by its authors' names, *Wright and Miller*, is an excellent guide on how to practice litigation in the federal courts. In addition to a detailed analysis of the rules that frame each step of the litigation process, *Wright and Miller* also includes forms, explanations, and citations to primary authority. This helpful resource can steer you through actions not only in Article III courts, but before Administrative Law Judges as well.

Wright and Miller also includes, as you can see, substantial information regarding Rule 4.

RULE 4. SUMMONS

Analysis

[In Volume 4]

A. SERVICE OF PROCESS AND PERSONAL JURISDICTION—IN GENERAL

Sec.
1061.   History and Purpose of Rule 4.
1062.   Service of Process Other Than as Explicitly Prescribed in Rule 4.
1063.   Subject Matter jurisdiction. Venue. Personal Jurisdiction, and Service of Process Distinguished.
1063.1 Hierarchy of Types of Jurisdiction.
1064.   Personal Jurisdiction—Traditional Dogma.
1065.   Personal Jurisdiction in Transition—Individuals.
1066.   ____ Corporations.
1067.   Modern Supreme Court Notions of Personal Jurisdiction—International Shoe.
1067.1 Supreme Court Development of Minimum Contacts Doctrine.
1067.2 Minimum Contacts, Fair Play, and Substantial Justice.
1067.3 Exceptions to Minimum Contacts Requirements.
1067.4 Volkswagen, Asahi, and Stream of Commerce Theory.
1067.5 General Jurisdiction.
1067.6 Procedural Aspects of Personal Jurisdiction.
1068.   Growth And Use of Long-Arm Statutes.
1068.1 Personal Jurisdiction in Federal Question Cases.

*   *   *

Treatises

Your practice continues to grow! Now, you have an assignment in which you must determine if the Clean Air Act applies to a certain set of facts.

You could just Google "Clear Air Act" and read the statute, but most statutes have been significantly interpreted by case law. You could look for the cases, but how do you know which cases are important? Again, rely on an expert. You find a book called *The Clean Air Act Handbook*. This is a **treatise**.

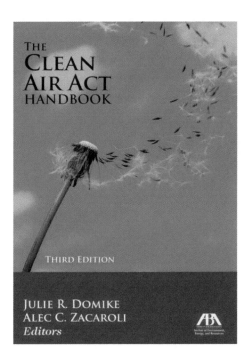

Treatises are detailed explanations of a particular area of law written by legal scholars or experienced practitioners. They can be single- or multi-volume. Although treatises are secondary sources, and therefore not the law, some treatises are known as the go-to source for getting up to speed in a given area (e.g. *Nimmer on Copyright* or *Williston on Contracts*).

*　　*　　*

Hornbooks

A variation on a treatise is a **hornbook**. Hornbooks are usually single volumes that explain one area of law in a more basic way than a treatise. They are written for law students to use as supplements to their casebooks. Because hornbooks are intended to be more simplified explanations of the law, they cite primarily to the landmark cases in that area, which make them useful when it is necessary to identify the must-cite cases.

Below is an example of a hornbook on legal research.

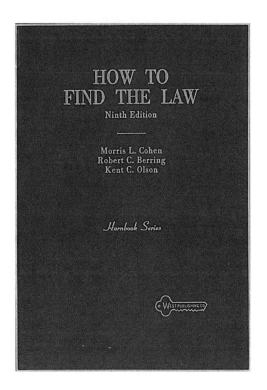

*　　*　　*

Law Journals

Occasionally you will be interested in seeing a more theoretical approach to a topic. For example, suppose you are writing a brief where you want to present a novel approach to the legal problem of whether clicking on a button on a website creates a binding contract. In this case you would want to look at a law journal or law review.

BOSTON UNIVERSITY

LAW REVIEW

PAP

ARTICLES

Plunging into Endless Difficulties: *Nicole Huberfeld,*
Medicaid and Coercion in *National*   *Elizabeth Weeks Leonard*
Federation of Independent Business v. Sebelius   *& Kevin Outterson*

Veil-Piercing Unbound   *Peter B. Oh*

ESSAY

The Impending iPrize Revolution in Intellectual
Property Law   *Saul Levmore*

NOTES

Taking Aim at Felony Possession   *Alexander C. Barrett*

The Commonwealth's Right to "Honest Services":
Prosecuting Public Corruption in Massachusetts   *Jared B. Cohen*

"Easing Out" the FCPA Facilitation Payment Exception   *Emily N. Strauss*

Volume 93   January 2013   Number 1

Law journals, or law reviews, contain scholarly articles examining a wide variety of legal issues. Law review articles are valuable not only for their depth, but also for the abundance of citations to both primary and secondary sources they provide. The two main ways to locate relevant journal articles are using an index and keyword searching. These methods will be discussed during the research method portion of this chapter.

Law Journals on HeinOnline

Of course, you can search for law journal articles on Westlaw or LexisNexis. Sometimes, though, it is better to use a lesser known resource called HeinOnline. Unlike Westlaw's and Lexis' law journal collections, which for most journals begin in the 1980s, HeinOnline contains PDFs of most law journal article dating back to the first volume. HeinOnline also has a more extensive collection of foreign and international legal journals. HeinOnline provides for basic keyword searching just like WestlawNext and Lexis Advance, and sorts its results by relevance. Although HeinOnline does not have quite as many connector options as WestlawNext and Lexis Advance, it does allow for proximity searching (within 5, 10, or 25 words) through its

Field Search. Ask a librarian if you would like to learn more about how to construct one of these searches. Another great feature of HeinOnline is that once you find a really great article, you can see other articles that have cited it, using the "Articles that cite this document" link.

* * *

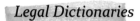
Legal Dictionaries

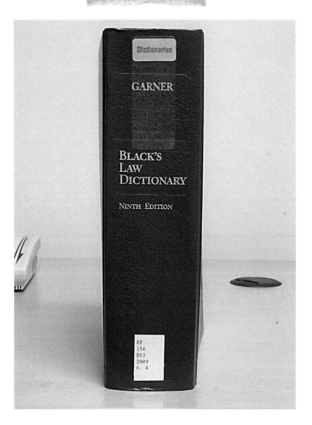

Legal dictionaries are a 1L's best friend because they provide plain meanings for legal terms. Popular legal dictionaries include *Black's Law Dictionary* and *Ballentine's Law Dictionary*. *Black's* is available on WestlawNext, and *Ballentine's* is available on Lexis Advance. Both are also available in print.

The electronic versions of these dictionaries allow you to search for the term you want defined. Once you locate the relevant entry in *Black's*, in addition to the definition, there will be links to relevant resources and key numbers.

Always use a legal dictionary when you encounter a term in a case or other resource that you do not understand.

*   *   *

Form Books

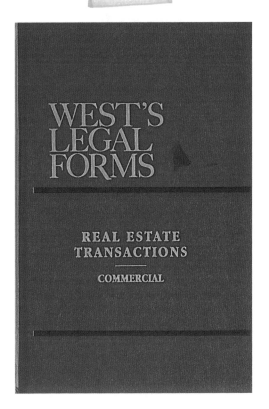

Form books are a valuable resource for practitioners. Just because you've never drafted an employment agreement does not mean you have to start from scratch (and, honestly, it's foolish to start from scratch). Forms are included in federal and state practice guides, and there are also entire series devoted to forms, such as *American Jurisprudence Legal Forms* and *West's Legal Forms*. The library also subscribes to looseleafs containing specialized forms, such as *Entertainment Industry Contracts: Negotiating and Drafting Guide*.

Try to avoid using transactional law forms that you find on the internet unless from a reputable source. Litigation forms can be found on court websites (always check for these). Forms are also available on Westlaw and LexisNexis.

Whenever you're drafting a document for the first time, don't reinvent the wheel; take advantage of the experience and knowledge of others. Use a form.

*   *   *

Restatements and Principles of the Law

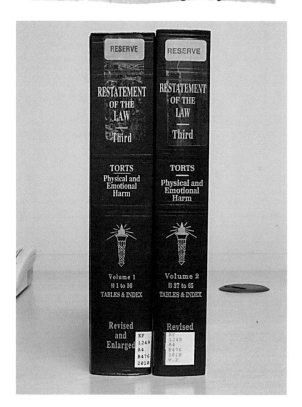

The Restatements and Principles of the Law series are published by the American Law Institute. The original purpose of the Restatements was to provide a concise statement of the prevailing common law rules in a particular legal area. This function is still true for many of the Restatements, but some also provide aspirational rules of law; that is, the direction the Restatement drafters believe the law should head in the future.[7] When the Restatements provide a summary of existing law, they can be a very persuasive secondary source.

---

[7]   *See, e.g.,* Jeremy Macklin, Comment, *The Puzzling Case of Max Feinberg: An Analysis of Conditions in Partial Restraint of Marriage,* 43 J. MARSHALL L. REV. 265, 274 n. 61 (2009).

There are currently Restatements and Principles of the Law in the following areas: Agency, Aggregate Litigation, Conflict of Laws, Contracts, Corporate Governance, Election Law, Employment Law, Family Dissolution, Foreign Relations Law of the United States, Intellectual Property, International Commercial Arbitration, Judgments, Law Governing Lawyers, Liability Insurance, Nonprofit Organizations, Property, Restitution and Unjust Enrichment, Security, Software Contracts, Suretyship and Guaranty, Torts, Transnational Civil Procedure, Transnational Insolvency, Trusts, and Unfair Competition.

* * *

Legal Thesauri

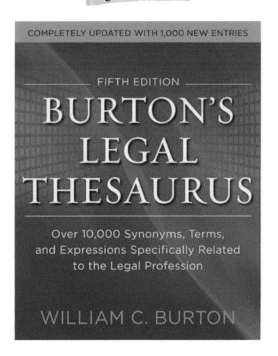

When you conduct legal research, either through an online keyword search or using an index, you will need to think of words that describe your legal problem. Because a judge or legislator may not use the exact same words, you need to think of synonyms to search for in addition to the terms you initially think of. A legal thesaurus can be useful to help you think of synonymous terms. New search terms are often found in other secondary sources as well.

* * *

Applying the Legal Research Method to Secondary Sources

Legal Research Method

1. Analyze problem and formulate key terms or concepts.

As noted in the Introduction, the first step in the legal research process is to analyze the problem at hand and think of keywords. Keywords are words or phrases that are essential to describing your factual situation. This involves examining the who, what, where, when, and why of your story.

2. Select a jurisdiction when searching for primary authority; know your jurisdiction when searching for secondary.

Applicable law is jurisdiction-specific, so it is important to know the relevant jurisdiction when researching.

3. Use key terms to search an index or a database.

Now that you have thought of your keywords, you need to use them in a finding tool, whether that's an index, table of contents, or search box, to find a relevant discussion in a secondary source. Although these finding methods are listed separately, keep in mind that you do not have to use one method exclusively as you research. It may be advantageous to combine methods, such as finding the appropriate section by using the index or table of contents, and then searching for a term within the section to quickly locate the portion of the article that speaks to your legal issue.

Using an Index

An index is a great way to find relevant portions of a secondary source, regardless of whether you're searching in print or online. Indexes are helpful because the editors are pointing you to meaningful discussions of a particular topic, whereas keyword searching may yield results where your search term is only mentioned in passing. The index is usually located at the end of the print volume, or is included as a separate link online, and the terms are organized alphabetically. When you use the index, you want to start by looking for your broadest keywords, and then look for the narrower keywords as subdivisions under the main heading. Once you find your narrow topic in the index, there will be an accompanying citation to a page or section within the main source. An example from *Massachusetts Practice* is below.

ANIMALS
Action against renter of horse, **V10-10C Proc Forms § 42:15**
Appropriations, **V18-18C Muni Law § 33.1**
Assets of estate, **V21-22 Probate § 26.4**
Beasts, replevin, **V17-17C Prima Fac § 49.2**
Breeding capacity, warranty, **V26-27B UCC Forms § 2-313—Form 21**
Complaints
   Dogbite
      Generally, **V10-10C Proc Forms § 42:13**
      Treble damages, **V10-10C Proc Forms § 42:14**
      Horse, vicious or dangerous, actions against owners and caretakers, **V10-10C Proc Forms § 42:15**
      Wild animals, actions against owners and keepers, **V10-10C Proc Forms § 42:18**

Table of Contents

The table of contents outlines the topics covered in a particular resource. Using the table of contents is an efficient way to research when you understand at least some of the terms associated with your legal issue. For example, if you wanted to research the law related to dog bites, you might know that issue falls within the larger topic of "Animals." You could then look up "Animals" in a table of contents and find the sections discussing liability for an injury caused by a dog. An example of such a table of contents from American Jurisprudence 2d is below.

AMERICAN JURISPRUDENCE 2D

   2.   Particular Kinds of Animals

      a. Dogs

§ 75 Generally
§ 76 Sufficiency of, and circumstances charging owner with, knowledge
§ 77 Fright causing bodily injury
§ 78 Liability imposed by statute
§ 79 —Persons liable; joint or several liability

      b. Horses

§ 80 Generally
§ 81 Injuries from being kicked, bitten, trampled, and the like by horse
§ 82 Injuries sustained by rider

      c. Other Animals

§ 83 Cats
§ 84 Bees

Keyword Searching

Keyword searching is likely the most popular method of legal research. It can be very effective, but don't discount other research methods like using an index or a table of contents (or even, gasp, researching in print). Keep in mind that a disadvantage of keyword searching is that you will often retrieve items where your term is mentioned only once and perhaps in a different context than you intended. Results from such a search may not be very helpful.

When keyword searching, we recommend that you always select a particular source or jurisdiction first.

4. Analyze Your Results

In all circumstances, you need to analyze your results to find helpful and relevant material. If your search is too broad, you can compensate by adding additional search terms or change "or" connectors to "and." If your search is too narrow, think of synonyms for your original search terms, and connect the similar terms with "or" connectors. If you find your search returned relevant results, it is time to read carefully to learn the context and standards applicable to your legal problem.

*   *   *

Working Through the Research Method with an Example

You represent a pharmaceutical company that already has a patent on a human drug. However, it would like to extend the life of its patent because FDA approval delayed its ability to market the drug when the patent first adhered.

1.   Analyze problem and formulate key terms or concepts.

The first step is to analyze the problem and formulate our key terms. Here, we want to know if it is possible for a pharmaceutical patent holder to extend the duration of its patent if it was not able to market the drug due to FDA approval delays. We know the broad area of law implicated is **patents**. In terms of "who" keywords, we know there is a patent owner and the **FDA**. For "what," we know that the covered invention is a **drug**, and that the company wants to **extend** the life (you might think of synonymous terms like **duration** or **term**) of its patent. The **delay** due to **FDA approval** is another likely legal significant "what" fact. "Where" and "why" are not really implicated by this factual scenario, except that patent law is primarily governed by federal law.

2. Select a jurisdiction when searching for primary authority; know your jurisdiction when searching for secondary.

The jurisdiction here is federal as it involves patents, which are subject to federal law, and the FDA, a federal agency.

3. Use key terms to search an index or a database.

Now that we have brainstormed some keywords, we need to look for them in our source. Because this is a patent issue, I chose an authoritative patent treatise, *Chisum on Patents*, which is available on LexisNexis. Within that source, I ran a keyword search using the terms **patent term extension drug FDA approval delay** in Lexis' *Chisum on Patents* database. The first three results are represented below:

1. Chisum on Patents, 5143 Patent Term Restoration

Chisum on Patents, Part III. Federal Circuit Guide, PART 1 TOPICAL OUTLINE WITH ABSTRACTS

(1) **PATENT** ON COMPOSITION OF INGREDIENTS; "FIRST COMMERCIAL MARKETING"; **PATENT TERM EXTENSION** EVALUATED ON "COMPONENT-BY-COMPONENT" BASIS. A **patent** claimed a composition comprising two ingredients, hydrocodone and ibuprofen. The **patent** owner obtained **FDA approval** to market a **drug** product covered by the **patent**. It applied to the PTO for restoration of **patent term** because of the **FDA** regulatory period. The PTO correctly denied restoration. Each of the ingredients (hydrocodone and ibuprofen) had …

2. 5-16 Chisum on Patents § 16.03

Chisum on Patents, Part I. Treatise on the Law of Patentability, Validity and Infringement, CHAPTER 16 Direct Infringement

… 982 F.2d at 1524 , 25 USPQ2d at 1199 . or legislative history. 192 The court noted: "The **Drug** Price Competition and **Patent Term** Restoration Act of 1984 … addressed two distinct problems created by the legal requirements for premarket **FDAapproval** of **drugs** and medical devices, and the lengthy **delays** often attendant on this **approval**. For products utilizing **patented** inventions, the **approval** process created problems at both ends of the **patent term**. "At the front end, a **patent**owner's …

3. 5-16 Chisum on Patents § 16.04

Chisum on Patents, Part I. Treatise on the Law of Patentability, Validity and Infringement, CHAPTER 16 Direct Infringement

… , its **term** was also extended to December 12, 2004. The **patent** owner sought **FDA approval** to market a **drug** (TRUSOPT®). It listed the '413 **patent** in the **FDA**'s "Orange Book" because the **patent** covered the **drug**. In 1997, the PTO granted the **patent** owner's request to extend the '413 **patent** 's **term** (1233 days) for a period of regulatory review for **approval** of TRUSOPT®. The PTO calculated the **extension** from the '413 **patent** 's reset terminal disclaimer date (December 12, 2004). Thus, the …

4. Analyze Your Results

The last step is to analyze our results. When I read the third search result, I learned about the ability to extend the term of a patent for a human drug under the Hatch-Waxman Act, and that is the most relevant and valuable secondary source on the list. The source will provide a background on the law, relevant considerations when seeking an extension, and helpful citations to primary authority. In other words, this is a great place to start my research!

*   *   *

Citing Secondary Sources

Books

Many secondary sources are cited as books. You should refer to Rule 15 of *The Bluebook* for more information on the proper formatting of author, title, page or section, editor, and publication year information. Examples of typical citations, with dots to delineate the spaces, are provided below. For these examples, notice that the volume number precedes the author's name, and section numbers are used in lieu of page numbers when available.

Hornbook Example

THOMAS • J. • SCHOENBAUM, • ADMIRALTY • AND • MARITIME • LAW • § • 7-29 • (5th • ed. • 2012).

Multivolume Treatise Example

26 • SAMUEL • WILLISTON • & • RICHARD • A. • LORD, • A • TREATISE • ON • THE • LAW • OF • CONTRACTS • § • 69:7 • (4th • ed. • 2003).

*   *   *

Rule 15.8(a) provides citation forms for common reference works, such as law dictionaries and legal encyclopedias, that would otherwise be cited as books. For the dictionary citation, note that the term itself is not mentioned in the citation. The citation below is for the term "guarantor," which appears on page 773 of the dictionary.

Law Dictionary Example

BLACK'S • LAW • DICTIONARY • 773 • (9th • ed. • 2009).

Legal Encyclopedia Example

7A • AM. • JUR. • 2D • *Automobile* • *Insurance* • § • 543 • (2007).

* * *

Restatements

Refer to Rule 12.9.5 when citing Restatements. The citation requires the title of the Restatement (abbreviated according to Table T6), the section number, and the year of publication. An example using white pages formatting appears below.

RESTATEMENT • (THIRD) • OF • FOREIGN • RELATIONS • § • 702 • (1987).

* * *

Law Review Articles

See Rule 16 to cite law review articles. Notice in the white pages example below that the authors' names are joined by an ampersand, and the second portion of the pin cite contains the last two digits of the page number.

Jan • P. • Charmatz • & • Harold • M. • Wit, • *Repatriation* • *of* • *Prisoners* • *of* • *War* • *and* • *the* • *1949* • *Geneva* • *Convention,* • 62 • YALE • L.J. • 391, • 391-94 • (1953).

* * *

Practice Questions

1. Which of the following citations is to a secondary source?
   a. 17 U.S.C. § 101 (2006 & Supp. V 2011).
   b. <u>Korea Supply Co. v. Lockheed Martin Corp.</u>, 63 P.3d 937 (Cal. 2003).
   c. 35A C.J.S. <u>Federal Civil Procedure</u> § 318 (2003).
   d. U.S. Const. amend. XIV, § 2.

2. You want to read a secondary source that discusses the factors Massachusetts courts consider when assigning property to divorcing parties. Which source would be most appropriate?
   a. Massachusetts Practice Series
   b. Corpus Juris Secundum
   c. American Jurisprudence 2d
   d. Black's Law Dictionary

3. Using the Table of Contents in *Federal Practice and Procedure*, find the section that discusses the rules for depositions in foreign countries.

4. Search in *Massachusetts Practice* on WestlawNext to find two sections that discuss the parent-child privilege, which provides that unemancipated minor children cannot be forced to testify against a parent in a criminal proceeding.

5. Using the *C.J.S.* index, find the section range where you can read about the need for a contract to be supported by consideration.

6. Using the *Am. Jur. 2d* table of contents, find a section discussing jury instructions during a criminal trial for bigamy.

7. Run a keyword search in *New York Jurisprudence 2d* to find the section with the title that will inform you what the acronym QTIP stands for.

8. You want to see which jurisdictions have adopted the "firefighter's rule," which prevents on-duty firefighters from suing property owners for personal injury resulting from the performance of firefighting duties. You would also like to learn about alternative approaches taken in other states. You know that *American Law*

Reports is a good source for comparing the different approaches taken by different jurisdictions. Search the *A.L.R.* for a relevant annotation.

9. You need to find a treatise on insurance law, but you don't know any relevant titles. Starting from the WestlawNext home page, what steps would you take to find one?

10. Use *Ballentine's Law Dictionary* to find the definition of "malice." What is the first definition provided?

11. Find a PDF of Professor Gordon's most-cited article: Wendy J. Gordon, *Fair Use as Market Failure: A Structural and Economic Analysis of the* Betamax *Case and Its Predecessors*, 82 COLUM. L. REV. 1600 (1982). Which online service did you use to find the PDF?

12. In the employment discrimination context, the ability of an employer to show it had a policy in place often goes a long way to help it avoid liability. The policies are often included in an employee handbook. As in-house counsel, it's your responsibility to make sure the handbook has the company covered. You've heard *Employment Discrimination Coordinator* is a great source for forms and checklists. Find a section that includes a checklist of questions to ask when reviewing the handbook.

13. Find the Uniform Trade Secrets Act. What is the title of § 4?

14. According to the Restatement (Second) of Contracts, can an intoxicated person ever avoid duties under a contract formed while he was intoxicated? Answer the question and provide the section you relied on.

15. What is the proper (blue pages) Bluebook citation for the answer to question 14?

Notes

Notes

Answer Key for Secondary Source Practice Questions

1. (c) 35A C.J.S. Federal Civil Procedure § 318 (2003).

2. (a) Massachusetts Practice Series
   Explanation: You always want to think about your jurisdiction when selecting a source. Because you are interested in the factors *Massachusetts* courts would apply, you want to search in a Massachusetts-specific resource. Although C.J.S. and Am. Jur. 2d also provide analysis, the scope of these resources is national. They may include citations to Massachusetts cases, but it is more efficient to start your research in a resource that is devoted to Massachusetts law.

3. § 2083

4. 19 Mass. Practice Evidence § 601.5 (2010).
   20 Mass. Practice Annotated Guide to Massachusetts Evidence § 504 (2010).

5. 17 C.J.S. Contracts §§ 99-167 (2011).

6. 11 Am. Jur. 2d Bigamy § 46 (2009).

7. 101 N.Y. Jur. 2d Taxation & Assessment § 2047 (2006).

8. Larry D. Scheafer, Annotation, *Liability of Owner or Occupant of Premises to Firefighter Coming Thereon in Discharge of His Duty*, 11 A.L.R. 4th 597 (1982).

9. Secondary Sources – By Topic: Insurance Law – Texts and Treatises

10. "A state of mind, being ill will, hatred, or hostility entertained by one person toward another."

11. HeinOnline

12. 7 Employment Discrimination Coordinator Forms, Pleadings and Practice Aids § 2:4 (2013).

13. Attorney's Fees
    Explanation: The Uniform Trade Secrets Act can be located in the Uniform Laws Annotated.

14. Yes, § 16

15. Restatement (Second) of Contracts § 16 (1981).

Researching Cases

Researching Cases

What is a Case?

A case is a written decision issued by a judge or panel of judges at either the trial court, intermediate appellate court, or supreme court level regarding a dispute between two or more parties. The decision generally resolves the entire dispute or single or multiple issue(s) that have arisen during the course of the dispute.

In resolving the dispute, the judge will state and bring to bear applicable legal principles. These principles will for the most part derive from federal or state statutory (or regulatory) sources or the common law. It is the judge's duty to apply these legal principles to the facts of the case before her.

* * *

The Federal and State Court Systems

Cases emanate from courts. The United States has one court system for the country as a whole (the federal system) and then parallel systems in each of the 50 states. Cases may be brought in either of the two systems. State courts generally can hear any case brought before them while federal courts are limited to hearing cases raising a question of federal law[8] or cases involving a dispute between citizens of different states, or between a citizen of a state and a citizen of a foreign country, where the amount in controversy exceeds $75,000.[9]

The organization of the federal and state systems is exactly parallel. Both systems consist of the following:

Trial Court (called the District Court in the federal system). The trial court is the first court in which a dispute, usually initiated with the filing of a complaint, is brought. This court, presided over by a single judge, will frame the dispute; shepherd the dispute through the pretrial process, which includes motion practice and the exchange of information between the parties (know as "discovery"); determine whether the case should go to trial;

---

[8] *See* 28 U.S.C. § 1331 (2006).

[9] *See* 28 U.S.C. § 1332 (2006).

and then at trial, generally with the aid of a jury as the finder of fact, resolve the dispute in favor of one of the parties.

Intermediate Appellate Court (called the Court of Appeals in the federal system). The party that loses in the trial court has an automatic right of appeal to the intermediate appellate court. Essentially, the losing party argues that the trial court did something wrong or "erred" in the application of the law to the facts, and if the appellate court were to correct this error, the losing party would end up the winner.

Supreme Court. The federal system and each state have a *supreme court*. A state supreme court is the final arbiter for all cases brought within its state (except for certain circumstances where a case from a state supreme court can be appealed to the United States Supreme Court). The United States Supreme Court is the final arbiter for all cases arising under federal law, including the United States Constitution, and the federal statutory and regulatory schemes. Parties have only a *discretionary* right of appeal from the intermediate appellate court to a supreme court. That means that a supreme court *chooses* the cases, usually those of particular importance with regard to the facts or the law, that it wants to hear.

*   *   *

Hierarchy of Case Authority

Cases are important to the parties to the dispute in question, of course, but also because they have *precedential* value. For our purposes, precedent means a "decided case that furnishes a basis for determining later cases involving similar facts or issues."[10] The decided case can be *binding precedent*,[11] which means a "precedent that a court must follow," because it is from a higher court within the same jurisdiction, or the decided case can be *persuasive precedent*, which is a "precedent that is not binding on a court, but that is entitled to respect and careful consideration."[12] This could be a decided case from a court at the same level in the same jurisdiction or from a court in a neighboring jurisdiction. Either way, the court is not

---

[10]   BLACK'S LAW DICTIONARY 1295 (9th ed. 2009).

[11]   *Id.* at 1296.

[12]   *Id.*

bound by the earlier case, but may use its reasoning in deciding the case before it.

For example, all federal trial courts in the First Circuit (covering Maine, Massachusetts, New Hampshire, Puerto Rico, and Rhode Island) *must* adhere to applicable precedent from the First Circuit Court of Appeals, as decisions from that court are binding precedent on them. On the other hand the federal trial court in the District of Massachusetts *may* follow the reasoning from a case in the District of Maine if it finds that reasoning persuasive. Similarly, all courts in the First Circuit, including the Court of Appeals, *must* adhere to precedent from the United States Supreme Court, and *may* follow persuasive precedent in the form of decided cases from outside the circuit if they choose.

Recognizing that cases have precedential value provides the key reason for why lawyers research and use them. Simply, lawyers look for prior decided cases that have outcomes favorable to their clients and that are most similar in terms of facts and legal issues to the situations facing their clients. Once these cases are located, the lawyer argues that the result in the earlier case, as either binding or persuasive precedent, should control or inform the outcome for her client in the present case.

In other words, the "best" case you can find is normally, (1) binding precedent from your jurisdiction that is (2) similar in facts and issues to your case, and (3) where the outcome of the case is favorable to your client. By "favorable outcome", I mean that if you're seeking dismissal of a case based on a particular issue, you want a case that dismisses on that issue, etc. Once you find that "best" case, simply compare it to your client's situation and argue that the outcome for your client should be the same as that in the earlier decided case.

*   *   *

Reporters

Cases are published in **reporters**. A **reporter** is a print set of books, organized by volume number, in which a particular jurisdiction's cases are collected in chronological order. There are separate reporter systems for the federal judiciary and also for each of the states. State cases are also published in **regional reporters**, which collect cases decided by the courts of several different states. Please see the charts beginning below for more information on reporters.

Federal Reporters

Reporter	Years Covered	Abbreviation
District Court		
Federal Supplement	1932-1998	F. Supp.
Federal Supplement 2d	1998-date	F. Supp. 2d
Federal Rules Decisions	1938-date	F.R.D.
West's Bankruptcy Reporter	1979-date	B.R.
Court of Appeals		
Federal Reporter	1891-1924	F.
Federal Reporter 2d	1924-1993	F.2d
Federal Reporter 3d	1993-date	F.3d
Federal Appendix (unpub cases)	2001-date	F. App'x
Supreme Court		
United States Reports (official reporter)	1790-date	U.S.
Supreme Court Reporter (unofficial; published by West)	1882-date	S. Ct.
Lawyer's Edition (unofficial; published by Lexis)	1790-date	L.Ed., L.Ed. 2d
United States Law Week	1933-date	U.S.L.W.

Reporter	Abbreviation	States Covered
Atlantic	A., A.2d, A.3d	CT, DC, DE, MD, ME, NH, NJ, PA, RI, VT
North Eastern	N.E., N.E.2d	IL, IN, MA, NY, OH
North Western	N.W., N.W.2d	IA, MI, MN, ND, NE, SD, WI
Pacific	P., P.2d, P.3d	AK, AZ, CA, CO, HI, ID, KS, MT, NM, NV, OK, OR, UT, WA, WY
Southern	So., So. 2d, So. 3d	AL, FL, LA, MS
South Eastern	S.E., S.E.2d	GA, NC, SC, VA, WV
South Western	S.W., S.W.2d, S.W.3d	AR, KY, MO, TN, TX

*   *   *

Citations to Cases

A case's **citation** consists of information following the name of the case that shows where the case can be found in the relevant print reporter, the court that decided the case, and when the case was decided. Examples of case citations are below. Make sure you know how to identify each component of the citation.

First is citation information from a case decided by the state intermediate appellate court in Pennsylvania. The dots indicate spaces.

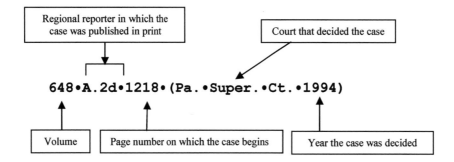

Next is a citation from the federal district court in Massachusetts.

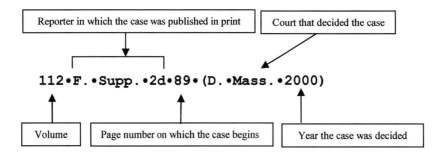

*   *   *

Parts of a Case

Cases, whether published in print or online, have several distinct parts of which you must be aware. They are:

1. **Caption.** A case's caption includes the "metadata" regarding the case. In particular, the caption includes the case name, the court that decided the case, the case's docket number, the case's citation in print (if any), and the date of the decision.

2. **Syllabus.** A case's syllabus is a brief summary of the case that immediately follows the caption. The syllabus is not written by the court and is not considered part of the case for precedential or citation purposes. The syllabus includes the specific holdings made by the court and the disposition of the matter that was before the court.

3. **Headnotes.** Headnotes follow the syllabus. Headnotes are brief summaries of specific points of law that are covered in the opinion. Headnotes are numbered. The points of law that the headnotes represent, as discussed below in detail, fit within a structure and organization of the law established by Westlaw and LexisNexis (each has established a different hierarchy; West's is older and generally considered the more useful). That being the case, only cases that you find on Westlaw or LexisNexis and the print reporters published by them will contain headnotes. As with the syllabus, headnotes are not written by the court and are not considered part of the decision for precedential or citation purposes.

4. **Attorneys and Judges.** Following the headnotes, you will find the names of the attorneys involved in the case and the judges that decided the case, including the name of the specific judge who wrote the opinion.

5. **Opinion.** Finally, comes the opinion, which is written by the court. It is the opinion that has precedential value and it is the only part of a case that should be cited.

An example from a West reporter, showing the initial parts of the case, begins on the next page. The parts of the case are the same whether you view the case online or in print.

Unless otherwise agreed among the parties, Co–Lead Plaintiffs shall file an amended consolidated class action complaint on or before 45 days from the date of entry of this order and opinion. Defendants shall submit any answer or defense thereto on or before 45 days after the filing of the amended consolidated class action complaint.

It is so ordered.

Caption

Laura ZUBULAKE, Plaintiff,

v.

UBS WARBURG LLC, UBS Warburg, and UBS Ag, Defendants.

No. 02 Civ. 1243(SAS).

United States District Court, S.D. New York.

July 20, 2004.

Background: Female employee brought suit against former employer for gender discrimination, failure to promote, and retaliation under federal, state, and city law. Plaintiff moved for sanctions for failure to produce relevant material and for tardy production of such material.

Holdings: The District Court, Scheindlin, J., held that:

(1) as sanction for plaintiff's destruction of relevant e-mails by defendant's employees in defiance of explicit instructions by counsel not to do so, jury would be given an adverse inference instruction with respect to those e-mails, and

(2) as sanction for tardy production of relevant e-mails, defendant would be required pay the costs of any depositions or re-depositions required by the late production, and to pay costs of plaintiff's motion for sanctions.

Motion granted.

End of Syllabus

1. **Federal Civil Procedure** ⟜1636.1

"Spoliation" is the destruction or significant alteration of evidence, or the failure to preserve property for another's use as evidence in pending or reasonably foreseeable litigation.

> See publication Words and Phrases for other judicial constructions and definitions.

2. **Evidence** ⟜78

The spoliation of evidence germane to proof of an issue at trial can support an inference that the evidence would have been unfavorable to the party responsible for its destruction.

3. **Federal Civil Procedure** ⟜1636.1, 2173

A party seeking an adverse inference instruction or other sanctions for the spoliation of evidence must establish the following three elements: (1) that the party having control over the evidence had an obligation to preserve it at the time it was destroyed; (2) that the records were destroyed with a culpable state of mind and (3) that the destroyed evidence was relevant to the party's claim or defense such that a reasonable trier of fact could find that it would support that claim or defense.

4. **Evidence** ⟜78

A "culpable state of mind" for purposes of a spoliation inference includes ordinary negligence.

> See publication Words and Phrases for other judicial constructions and definitions.

5. **Federal Civil Procedure** ⟜1636.1

When evidence is destroyed in bad faith, i.e., intentionally or willfully, that fact alone is sufficient to demonstrate relevance for purpose of sanction for spoliation of evidence; by contrast, when the destruction is negligent, relevance must be proven by the party seeking the sanctions.

Headnotes and Key Numbers

As noted above, headnotes are brief summaries of points of law discussed in a case that are compiled by the legal publishers West and LexisNexis. To understand headnotes, it is important to understand the basic challenge faced by lawyers in the late 19th century – namely, there was an ever increasing number of cases being decided, all of which were published chronologically in print reporters with few ways, other than reading every case or at least part of every case, to determine if a particular case was relevant to a particular client's situation. There was no searching. There was no way to research cases by subject matter.

In response to this challenge, John B. West, the founder of West Publishing created the "American Digest Classification Scheme" in the 1880s.[13] The "scheme" relied on the division of American law into over 400 major topic areas, like Appeal and Error, Commerce, Federal Civil Procedure, Monopolies, Patents, etc. The major topic areas were further subdivided into ever more specific subtopics. Each subtopic represented a specific point of law. When a case discussed that point of law, it was labeled with the relevant subtopic, thus collecting all cases that discussed the specific point of law under the same subtopic.

The way the scheme works today is this: when a published opinion is issued in a case, it is reviewed by an editor at West (and LexisNexis, which has a parallel system), and the editor determines the key legal issues decided or discussed in the case. Each of these legal issues is then placed under one of the major topics in the classification, and ultimately under one of the more specific subtopics. The specific subtopics are each given a number, called by West a "Key Number", to serve as a short hand notation for the subtopic. The editor then drafts a brief description of the legal issues involved and that description is placed before the actual opinion as a headnote. An example of a headnote is on the next page.

---

[13]   Robert M. Jarvis, *John B. West: Founder of the West Publishing Company*, 50 AM. J. LEGAL HIST. 1, 8 (2008-10).

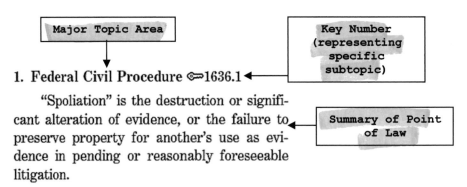

1. Federal Civil Procedure ⌖1636.1

"Spoliation" is the destruction or significant alteration of evidence, or the failure to preserve property for another's use as evidence in pending or reasonably foreseeable litigation.

See publication Words and Phrases for other judicial constructions and definitions.

2. Evidence ⌖78

The spoliation of evidence germane to proof of an issue at trial can support an inference that the evidence would have been unfavorable to the party responsible for its destruction.

This process is repeated for every case and applied consistently. So, *every* case that discusses the legal issue that falls under **Evidence and key number 78** (using the example from above) has the same headnote, and is assigned that topic and key number.

This provides a method for researching cases by topic and legal issue rather than full-text searching. The various legal issues, topics, key numbers, and summaries are collected in books specific to each jurisdiction called "digests." So, to find all cases that have the same legal issue as noted in **Evidence k.78**, simply browse to that topic and key number in the digest (it's ordered alphanumerically). There you will find other cases that discuss the legal issue that interests you. An example of a digest entry is below.

Evidence k.78

C.A.9 (Hawai'i) 1991. Generally, trier of fact may draw adverse inference from destruction of evidence relevant to the case.
    Akiona v. U.S., 938 F.2d 158, certiorari denied, 112 S.Ct. 1567, 503 U.S. 962, 118 L.Ed.2d 212.

Why is this important? Well, there are several reasons. First, headnotes can provide a useful summary of the law discussed in the case so that a case's relevance can be judged quickly, just by glancing at the headnotes. Second, using headnotes permits researching by subject, rather than full-text. That means all the cases surveyed under a particular topic and key number will involve the same legal issue, permitting a scan of relevant case law across jurisdictions. And third, use of headnotes, topics, and key numbers allows the researcher to find relevant cases using "one good case." More on that below.

*   *   *

Finding Cases Using "One Good Case"

As noted above, headnotes and key numbers permit classification of cases by the legal issues they discuss. Thus, every case that discusses an adverse inference flowing from spoliation (destruction of evidence) will have a headnote titled **Evidence k.78** (see above). This provides a very useful research technique once you find a case that supports your position; that is, once you find a "good case."

Here's how it works. Say you are in a situation where you suspect that the other side has destroyed evidence, and you want to know what type of remedy there is for that. A colleague knows something about this issue and shows you the case of *Akiona v. U.S.* from the Ninth Circuit Court of Appeals, which discusses destruction of evidence (case is referenced in digest example, above). The problem is that you are practicing in federal court in Pennsylvania, which is in the Third Circuit, and thus the Ninth Circuit case isn't binding authority. Is there a way to find relevant cases in your jurisdiction using that Ninth Circuit case?

You bet, and it's easy. In print, just go to the digest covering the federal courts and look up **Evidence k.78** (relating to destruction of evidence). All the Third Circuit cases will be collected together under that topic and key number. Just find the best case out of that batch and, suddenly, you're a hero!

It's even easier online. The headnotes on Westlaw and LexisNexis are all linked in such a way that clicking on the headnote or topic and key number will direct you to all cases that have that topic and key number. An intervening screen permits you to filter your results by jurisdiction. What could be easier than that? See the screen shots beginning on the next page for examples.

Here's an example of a West Headnote. "Antitrust and Trade Regulation" and "Courts" are the major topic areas. Beneath those labels is the summary of the specific point of law involved. To the right is the topic and subtopic hierarchy, showing the specific subtopics under the major topics. "Sports" is the most specific subtopic under Antitrust and Trade Regulation.

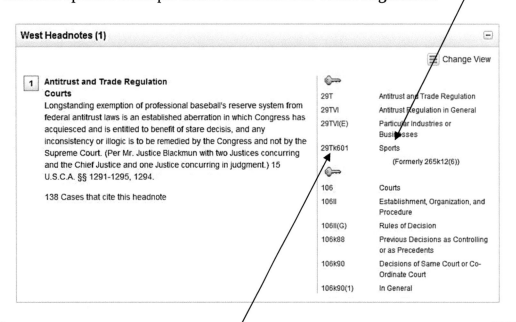

Selecting the key number link 29Tk601 will collect all cases with that specific key number, in other words all cases about Sports and Antitrust (29T stands for the major topic area, "Antitrust and Trade Regulation"; k601 is key number 601, standing for "Sports"). The results are below, filtered to show only those cases decided by the United States Supreme Court (only the first case (of eight) is shown).

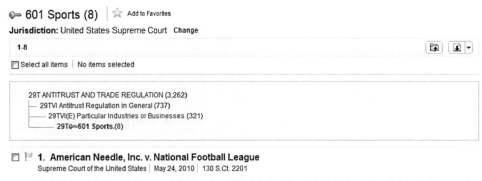

The same headnote from the same case is shown below using the system created by LexisNexis. Here there are no key numbers, just subtopics. The most specific subtopic is Baseball.

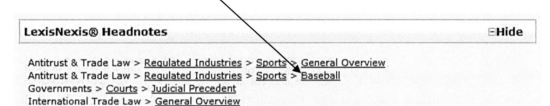

> ### LexisNexis® Headnotes ⊟Hide
>
> Antitrust & Trade Law > Regulated Industries > Sports > General Overview
> Antitrust & Trade Law > Regulated Industries > Sports > Baseball
> Governments > Courts > Judicial Precedent
> International Trade Law > General Overview
>
> **_HN1_** Professional baseball is a business and it is engaged in interstate commerce. With its reserve system enjoying exemption from the federal antitrust laws, baseball is, in a very distinct sense, an exception and an anomaly. Even though others might regard this as unrealistic, inconsistent, or illogical, the aberration is an established one. It is an aberration that has been with us now for half a century, one heretofore deemed fully entitled to the benefit of stare decisis, and one that has survived the court's expanding concept of interstate commerce. It rests on a recognition and an acceptance of baseball's unique characteristics and needs. Other professional sports operating interstate are not so exempt. _Shepardize - Narrow by this Headnote_
>
> Antitrust & Trade Law > Regulated Industries > Sports > General Overview
>
> **_HN2_** Since 1922 baseball, with full and continuing congressional awareness, has been allowed to develop and to expand unhindered by federal legislative action. Remedial legislation has been introduced repeatedly in Congress but none has ever been enacted. The court, accordingly, has concluded that Congress as yet has had no intention to subject baseball's reserve system to the reach of the antitrust statutes. This, obviously, has been deemed to be something other than mere congressional silence and passivity. _Shepardize - Narrow by this Headnote_
>
> Antitrust & Trade Law > Regulated Industries > Sports > General Overview
> Antitrust & Trade Law > Regulated Industries > Sports > Baseball

Selecting "Baseball" will bring up cases regarding Antitrust and Baseball.

In sum, the headnote system classifies cases by topic. That means that once you find a case with a topic that interests you, you can find many similar cases just by using a digest and looking up that topic or clicking on the headnote link provided in Westlaw and LexisNexis. This can be a very efficient way to research.

*   *   *

Finding a Case by Citation or Party Name

As noted, cases have both citations and names (the case name normally includes the names of the parties involved), and if you know one or both, it is typically quite easy to find the case in question.

In print, finding a case by citation involves nothing more than pulling the correct reporter volume from the shelf and turning to the proper page number. Finding a case by party name (again in print) is scarcely more difficult. To do that, use the Table of Cases, which is part of the digest system in every jurisdiction, and look the case up alphabetically by either party's name. That will give you the case's citation, permitting you to find the case quickly. An excerpt from the Table of Cases for the Federal Practice Digest 4th is below.

As far as online finding tools go, Westlaw and LexisNexis both offer efficient tools for finding a case by citation or party name.

For Westlaw, simply enter the case name or citation into the main search box. You need to make sure to select the proper jurisdiction. For Lexis, you would do the same. Clicking "Search" will retrieve the case.

*　　*　　*

Searching for Cases on Westlaw and LexisNexis

This section will discuss solving case law research problems involving different levels of complexity by *searching* on Westlaw and LexisNexis.

One of the most basic types of case law research problems is the "single issue" problem. This type of problem involves finding the key case on a single issue. Examples of these research problems are below.

- Find the United States Supreme Court case on corporate spending and political speech in elections.

- Find the New York case authored by then Chief Justice Cardozo on causation in tort cases in the context of an accident on a railroad platform.

- Find the federal bankruptcy case involving Bernie Madoff's investment company.

With questions like these, even though the problem is merely "single issue," the research method discussed previously remains the same. Below is application of the method using the first example on corporate spending and political speech.

1. **Analyze problem and formulate key terms or concepts.**

The key concepts here are two; "corporate spending" and "political speech." These will be our search terms.

2. **Select a jurisdiction when searching for primary authority; know your jurisdiction when searching for secondary.**

The jurisdiction or court here is the United States Supreme Court.

3. **Use key terms to search an index or a database.**

Now, using our key terms, it's time search in the relevant database, which is that for the Supreme Court.

4. **Analyze results.**

The first three results from searching in the Westlaw Supreme Court database are represented below.

1. ## Citizens United v. Federal Election Com'n

   Supreme Court of the United States January 21, 2010 558 U.S. 310

   CIVIL RIGHTS - Free **Speech**. **Corporations** have First Amendment **political speech** rights.

   ... **Corporate speech**, however, is derivative **speech**, **speech** by proxy....

   ... Differential treatment of media **corporations** and other **corporations** cannot be squared with the First Amendment, and there is no support for the view that the Amendment's original meaning would permit suppressing media **corporations' political speech**....

2. ## Buckley v. Valeo

   Supreme Court of the United States January 30, 1976 424 U.S. 1

   Various candidates for federal office and **political** parties and organizations brought action challenging constitutionality of Federal Election Campaign Act. The District Court for the...

   ...results of a primary held for the selection of delegates to a national nominating convention of a **political** party or for the expression of a preference for the nomination of persons for election to the office of President of the United States;(2) means a contract, promise, or agreement, express or implied, whether or not legally enforceable, to make any expenditure; and(3) means the transfer of...

3. ## McConnell v. Federal Election Com'n

   Supreme Court of the United States December 10, 2003 540 U.S. 93

   GOVERNMENT - Elections. Bipartisan Campaign Reform Act of 2002 was generally upheld as constitutional.

   ... Justice KENNEDY accuses us of engaging in a sleight of hand by conflating "unseemly **corporate speech**" with the **speech** of **political**parties and candidates, and then adverting to the "**corporate speech** rationale as if it were the linchpin of the case." ...

The first case, *Citizens United*, is the one we're looking for.

See how it works? Please try the other single-issue examples yourself. If you have any difficulties, please see your instructor or a librarian.

A second common case law research question is the "elements" question; that is, the lawyer or student is asked to find the elements of a particular cause of action or crime. This type of question is extremely important to a litigator or trial lawyer as it defines the claim the lawyer must ultimately prove or defend against and defeat. Examples of this type of question are below.

- Find the elements for a claim of fraud under Massachusetts law.

- Find the elements for a claim of copyright infringement under federal law.

- Find the elements for the crime of burglary under Michigan law.

Here too, we use the four-step research method.

1.   Analyze problem and formulate key terms or concepts.

In the first example, the key concepts/search terms are "fraud" and "elements."

2.   Select a jurisdiction when searching for primary authority; know your jurisdiction when searching for secondary.

The proper jurisdiction is Massachusetts.

3.   Use key terms to search an index or a database.

We will search using the terms "fraud" and "elements" in the Massachusetts case law database.

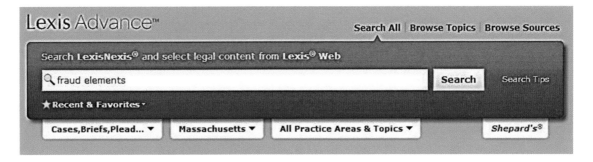

4.   Analyze results.

The first three results from the LexisNexis Massachusetts cases database are shown below.

1. **Ⓐ Ward v. Costello, 15 Mass. L. Rep. 644**

   The **elements** required to prove **fraud** in the inducement are: (1) a misrepresentation of material fact, (2) made to induce action, (3) and reasonable reliance on the false statement to the detriment of the actor. Reliance is an **element** of actionable **fraud**. The **elements** required to prove **fraud** in the inducement are: (1) a misrepresentation of material fact, (2) made to induce action, (3) and reasonable reliance on the false statement to the detriment of the actor. See Commerce Bank & Trust Co. v. ...

2. **Venture Inv. Partners, LLC v. JT Venture Partners, LLC, 23 Mass. L. Rep. 304**

   Count Three asserts a claim for intentional misrepresentation. The defendants are correct that the Complaint does not plead--indeed, would seem to negate--the necessary **element** of reliance in connection with the alleged overvaluation of Hyperchip. 9 The Complaint alleges that other investors were duped into responding to the capital call for the Hyperchip investment and that VIP, though it did not so respond, was nonetheless damaged through the forfeiture of 25% of its interest. Delaware ...

3. **◆ Macoviak v. Chase Home Mortg. Corp., 40 Mass. App. Ct. 755**

   ... The affidavit from the plaintiff's expert witness only states that witness's opinion that Fidelity was negligent in preparing the appraisal report, not that it was wilful. Proof of negligence does not establish willfulness to fulfill the "intent" **element** of **fraud**. Proof of negligence does not establish wilfulness to fulfill the "intent" **element** of **fraud**.

The first case looks helpful. Read it.

The first case is helpful. It sets forth the elements of fraud and provides citations to cases that may also be helpful. Please see the excerpt from the case below.

_**HN5**_ The **elements** required to prove **fraud** in the inducement are: (1) a misrepresentation of material fact, (2) made to induce action, (3) and reasonable reliance on the false statement to the detriment of the actor. See _Commerce Bank & Trust Co. v. Hayeck_, 46 Mass. App. Ct. 687, 692, 709 N.E.2d 1122 (1999), citing _Hogan v. Riemer_, 35 Mass.App.Ct. 360, 365, 619 N.E.2d 984 (1993). "Reliance is an **element** of actionable **fraud**." _Nei v. Burley_, 388 Mass. 307, 311, 446 N.E.2d 674 (1983), citing _Kilroy v. Barron_, 326 Mass. 464, 465, 95 N.E.2d 190 (1950).

Finally, there is the legal research question that generally involves the lawyer trying to solve or analyze a complex problem presented by a client. An example is below.

Marlo Mackintosh is a famous celebrity. As such, she spends a large part of her day "tweeting" photos and descriptions of her various activities to her smallish cohort of followers. Actually, this is pretty much all she does. Anyway, Marlo has sought your counsel regarding her greatest fear; the dreaded "retweet." That is, she fears that some of her paltry band of somewhat loving followers are unscrupulous and will attempt to publish her tweeted photos without attribution or payment. Marlo wants to know what rights she has in her tweeted photos and whether she can stop others from publishing them. Research Marlo's question using federal law. And hurry! Marlo is just dying to tweet photos from her latest mani-pedi to her really-not-that-big-at-all cluster of, let's be frank now, thoroughly indifferent-to-her followers.

1.   Analyze problem and formulate key terms or concepts.

The key concepts/search terms here are "Twitter" and/or "retweet"; as well as "photo" or "photograph" and "copyright protection."

2.   Select a jurisdiction when searching for primary authority; know your jurisdiction when searching for secondary.

The relevant jurisdiction is federal law.

3.   Use key terms to search an index or a database.

Again, the key point at this step is to ensure that you are searching using the proper filters. You can see from below that your search for Marlo is filtered to retrieve only federal cases. As noted previously, you can also use the filters to select individual states, individual courts within a state, or individual courts within the federal system. The filters can also be set to search particular types of material, like statutes, cases, regulations, and even individual secondary sources.

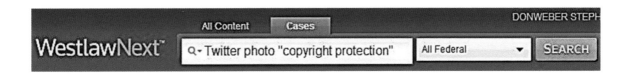

## 4.	Analyze results.

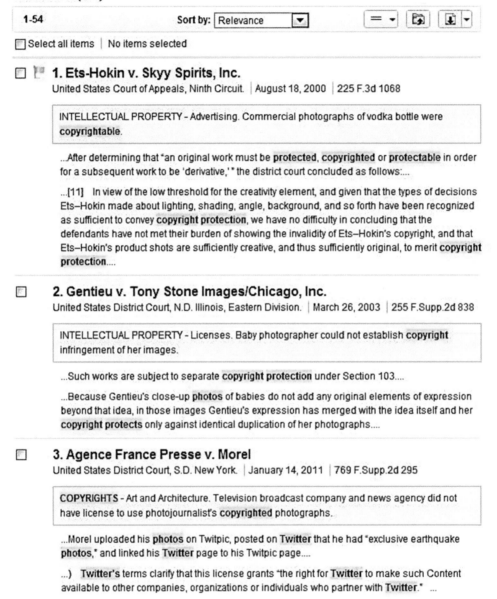

Cases (54)

| 1-54 | Sort by: Relevance ▼ | = ▼ ⊡ ⬇ ▼ |

☐ Select all items | No items selected

☐ ⚑ **1. Ets-Hokin v. Skyy Spirits, Inc.**
United States Court of Appeals, Ninth Circuit. | August 18, 2000 | 225 F.3d 1068

> INTELLECTUAL PROPERTY - Advertising. Commercial photographs of vodka bottle were **copyrightable**.

...After determining that "an original work must be **protected**, **copyrighted** or **protectable** in order for a subsequent work to be 'derivative,'" the district court concluded as follows:...

...[11] In view of the low threshold for the creativity element, and given that the types of decisions Ets–Hokin made about lighting, shading, angle, background, and so forth have been recognized as sufficient to convey **copyright protection**, we have no difficulty in concluding that the defendants have not met their burden of showing the invalidity of Ets–Hokin's copyright, and that Ets–Hokin's product shots are sufficiently creative, and thus sufficiently original, to merit **copyright protection**....

☐ **2. Gentieu v. Tony Stone Images/Chicago, Inc.**
United States District Court, N.D. Illinois, Eastern Division. | March 26, 2003 | 255 F.Supp.2d 838

> INTELLECTUAL PROPERTY - Licenses. Baby photographer could not establish **copyright** infringement of her images.

...Such works are subject to separate **copyright protection** under Section 103....

...Because Gentieu's close-up **photos** of babies do not add any original elements of expression beyond that idea, in those images Gentieu's expression has merged with the idea itself and her **copyright protects** only against identical duplication of her photographs....

☐ **3. Agence France Presse v. Morel**
United States District Court, S.D. New York. | January 14, 2011 | 769 F.Supp.2d 295

> COPYRIGHTS - Art and Architecture. Television broadcast company and news agency did not have license to use photojournalist's **copyrighted** photographs.

...Morel uploaded his **photos** on Twitpic, posted on **Twitter** that he had "exclusive earthquake **photos**," and linked his **Twitter** page to his Twitpic page....

...) **Twitter's** terms clarify that this license grants "the right for **Twitter** to make such Content available to other companies, organizations or individuals who partner with **Twitter**." ...

I chose the third case as it is the most recently decided (generally, a pretty good rule of thumb).

And, it was a good choice. The case expressly states that tweeted photographs are protected by copyright and cannot be republished without the photographer's permission.

Practice Questions

1. In which West regional reporters will you find the cases for the following states?

    A.   Pennsylvania
    B.   Tennessee
    C.   Massachusetts
    D.   Illinois
    E.   Vermont
    F.   South Carolina

2. Find 40 S. Ct. 17 and answer the following questions about the case.

    A.   What is the name of the case?

    B.   When was the case decided?

    C.   Who delivered the Court's opinion?

    D.   Were there any concurring or dissenting opinions in the case? Who wrote them? Give the full names of all Justices that dissented or concurred, and please state which opinions they dissented from or concurred in.

    E.   Is 40 S. Ct. 17 the official citation for this case? If not, what is?

    F.   How many headnotes are there?

3. Find 157 F.3d 191 and answer the following questions about the case.

    A.   What is the full citation of the case?

    B.   What is the name of the court that decided this case?

    C.   Who wrote the opinion of the court?

D. List the different topics noted in the headnotes and their key numbers.

E. The case involved two different Federal Rules of Civil Procedure. Name them. (HINT: Look at the first sentence of the court's opinion).

4. Find the missing portions of the following citations.

A. _____, 649 F.2d 894 (_____ 1981).

B. *Roberts v. Southwick*, _____ Mass. _____ (_____).

C. *Bushong v. Garman Co.*, _____ S.W.2d _____ (Ark. _____).

D. _____, 477 So. 2d 963 (_____).

5. Find 648 A.2d 1218 and answer the following questions about the case.

A. Give the full citation for this case.

B. If there is a parallel citation for this case, please provide it.

C. In what court was this case decided?

D. What is the specific relief that the court ordered?

6. In what Supreme Court of the United States case did the great Cardinal's center fielder Curt Flood challenge baseball's "reserve clause."

A. What is the name and official citation to the case?

B.   On what 2 Supreme Court cases is the Court's decision based?

C.   To what team did Flood object to being traded?

7.   In 2006, the New York Court of Appeals ruled that same-sex couples are not entitled to marry under state law.

A.   What is the name of this case?

B.   Where can the case be found in the North Eastern Reporter?

C.   Who authored the opinion?

D.   Suppose that you believe this case is directly related to your client's legal question, and you want to cite it as legal authority. You therefore decide to update the case to make sure that it is still currently valid. Is it still good law?

E.   Please identify 2 cases from the highest courts of other states that treat this case negatively. Please provide the citation and the holding for both cases.

8.   Your friend has been arrested for begging without a license in Harvard Square. Can you find a case that will help him? If so, give the full citation to that case.

Notes

Notes

Answers to Researching Cases Practice Questions

1. In which West regional reporters will you find the cases for the following states?

    A. Pennsylvania -- **Atlantic**
    B. Tennessee – **South Western**
    C. Massachusetts -- **Northeastern**
    D. Illinois -- **Northeastern**
    E. Vermont -- **Atlantic**
    F. South Carolina – **South Eastern**

2. Find 40 S. Ct. 17 and answer the following questions about the case.

    A. What is the name of the case?
        Abrams v. United States

    B. When was the case decided?
        November 10, 1919

    C. Who delivered the Court's opinion?
        Justice Clarke

    D. Were there any concurring or dissenting opinions in the case? Who wrote them? Give the full names of all Justices that dissented or concurred, and please state which opinions they dissented from or concurred in.
        Justice Holmes dissented from the opinion of the Court
        Justice Brandeis concurred in Holmes' dissent

    E. Is 40 S. Ct. 17 the official citation for this case? If not, what is?
        No. <u>Abrams v. United States</u>, 250 U.S. 616 (1919).

    F. How many headnotes are there?
        5

3.   Find 157 F.3d 191 and answer the following questions about the case.

    A.   What is the full citation of the case?
            McCurdy v. American Board of Plastic Surgery, 157 F.3d 191 (3d Cir. 1998).

    B.   What is the name of the court that decided this case?
            United States Court of Appeals for the Third Circuit

    C.   Who wrote the opinion of the court?
            Judge Sloviter

    D.   List the different topics noted in the headnotes and their key numbers.

Federal Courts	**k763.1**
Federal Civil Procedure	**k534**
Federal Civil Procedure	**k536**
Federal Courts	**k146**
Federal Courts	**k813**
Federal Civil Procedure	**k417**

    E.   The case involved two different Federal Rules of Civil Procedure. Name them. (HINT: Look at the first sentence of the court's opinion).
            Rule 4(m)
            Rule 12(h)

4.   Find the missing portions of the following citations.

    A.   **<u>Riegel Textile Corp. v. Celanese Corp.</u>**, 649 F.2d 894 (**<u>2d Cir.</u>** 1981).

    B.   *Roberts v. Southwick*, **<u>415</u>** Mass. **<u>465</u>** (**<u>1993</u>**).

    C.   *Bushong v. Garman Co.*, **<u>843</u>** S.W.2d **<u>807</u>** (Ark. **<u>1992</u>**).

    D.   **<u>E.R. Squibb & Sons, Inc. v. Cox</u>**, 477 So. 2d 963 (**<u>Ala. 1985</u>**).

5. Find 648 A.2d 1218 and answer the following questions about the case.

   A. Give the full citation for this case.
      Acme Markets, Inc. v. Federal Armored Express, Inc., 648 A.2d 1218 (Pa. Super. Ct. 1994).

   B. If there is a parallel citation for this case, please provide it.
      437 Pa. Super. 41

   C. In what court was this case decided?
      Pennsylvania Superior Court

   D. What is the specific relief that the court ordered?
      Reversed the order of the lower court. Remanded the case for further proceedings.

6. In what Supreme Court of the United States case did the great Cardinal's center fielder Curt Flood challenge baseball's "reserve clause."

   A. What is the name and official citation to the case?
      Flood v. Kuhn, 407 U.S. 258 (1972).

   B. On what 2 Supreme Court cases is the Court's decision based?
      Federal Baseball Club v. National League, 259 U.S. 200 (1922).
      Toolson v. New York Yankees, 346 U.S. 356 (1953).

   C. To what team did Flood object to being traded?
      Philadelphia Phillies

7. In 2006, the New York Court of Appeals ruled that same-sex couples are not entitled to marry under state law.

   A. What is the name of this case?
      Hernandez v. Robles

B. Where can the case be found in the North Eastern Reporter?
855 N.E.2d 1

C. Who authored the opinion?
R.S. Smith

D. Suppose that you believe this case is directly related to your client's legal question, and you want to cite it as legal authority. You therefore decide to update the case to make sure that it is still currently valid. Is it still good law?
Yes, although called into doubt.

E. Please identify 2 cases from the highest courts of other states that treat this case negatively. Please provide the citation and the holding for both cases.
In re Marriage Cases, 43 Cal. 4th 757 (2008).
Kerrigan v. Commissioners of Public Health, 289 Conn. 135 (2008).

8. Your friend has been arrested for begging without a license in Harvard Square. Can you find a case that will help him? If so, give the full citation to that case.
Benefit v. City of Cambridge, 424 Mass. 918, 679 N.E.2d 184 (1997)

Researching Statutes

Researching Statutes

Statutory Research

In the hierarchy of legal sources, statutes come right after constitutions in order of authority. This is true whether you are in a state or in the federal system. If the area of law you are researching involves a statute you should first look at the language of the statute before you move on to cases interpreting the statute. How do you know there is a statute involved? This is mainly a question on the state level because federal law will always involve either a statute or the U.S. Constitution. On the state level there are some areas of law you will come to know typically involve statutes. Examples include family law, insurance law, tax law, vehicle law – any area of law where the state has found it more effective to make explicit that which may at one time have been embodied in case law. Case law, on the other hand, tends to cover property law, tort law, contract law, and those legal concepts that are older and relate to relationships. In most cases, however, you will not **know** there is a statute involved in regulating the area you are researching unless you do some background reading in secondary sources first. And even if you know there is a statute you will often not know what it is. So what are statutes and how do you find them?

*   *   *

What is a Statute?

Statutes are laws passed by legislative bodies, whether federal or state. The federal legislature—the United States Congress—passes laws during legislative sessions. Each session lasts two years.

Statutes are generally published in two forms, first as a session law and then as a code. The session law is the law or Act exactly as passed by the legislature. Session laws at the federal level are published in chronological order of passage in the *United States Statutes at Large*. The federal session laws are called *public laws*, and identified as follows: **Public Law No. 111-148**, which refers to the 148th law passed in the 111th session of Congress. Most federal session laws have a name, like, for example, the Immigration and Naturalization Act of 1952 (INA). This name is known as the session law's popular name. Federal session laws are also identified by where they are published in the Statutes at Large; for example, **61 Stat. 637**.

UNITED STATES
STATUTES AT LARGE

CONTAINING THE

LAWS AND CONCURRENT RESOLUTIONS
ENACTED DURING THE FIRST SESSION OF THE
ONE HUNDRED ELEVENTH CONGRESS
OF THE UNITED STATES OF AMERICA

2009

Because session laws are published in chronological order and likely contain sections involving different subject areas, they do not lend themselves to successful legal research. For that reason, following passage by the legislature, a session law is *codified* and placed in a *code*, like, for example, the *United States Code* (U.S.C.). Codes are organized by subject. At the federal level, the United States Code is organized into 51 titles or subject areas. The 51 titles are as follows:

- TITLE 1 - GENERAL PROVISIONS
- TITLE 2 - THE CONGRESS
- TITLE 3 - THE PRESIDENT
- TITLE 4 - FLAG AND SEAL, SEAT OF GOVERNMENT, AND THE STATES
- TITLE 5 - GOVERNMENT ORGANIZATION AND EMPLOYEES
- TITLE 6 - DOMESTIC SECURITY
- TITLE 7 - AGRICULTURE
- TITLE 8 - ALIENS AND NATIONALITY
- TITLE 9 - ARBITRATION
- TITLE 10 - ARMED FORCES
- TITLE 11 - BANKRUPTCY
- TITLE 12 - BANKS AND BANKING
- TITLE 13 - CENSUS
- TITLE 14 - COAST GUARD
- TITLE 15 - COMMERCE AND TRADE
- TITLE 16 - CONSERVATION
- TITLE 17 - COPYRIGHTS
- TITLE 18 - CRIMES AND CRIMINAL PROCEDURE
- TITLE 19 - CUSTOMS DUTIES
- TITLE 20 - EDUCATION
- TITLE 21 - FOOD AND DRUGS
- TITLE 22 - FOREIGN RELATIONS AND INTERCOURSE
- TITLE 23 - HIGHWAYS
- TITLE 24 - HOSPITALS AND ASYLUMS

- TITLE 25 - INDIANS
- TITLE 26 - INTERNAL REVENUE CODE
- TITLE 27 - INTOXICATING LIQUORS
- TITLE 28 - JUDICIARY AND JUDICIAL PROCEDURE
- TITLE 29 - LABOR
- TITLE 30 - MINERAL LANDS AND MINING
- TITLE 31 - MONEY AND FINANCE
- TITLE 32 - NATIONAL GUARD
- TITLE 33 - NAVIGATION AND NAVIGABLE WATERS
- TITLE 35 - PATENTS
- TITLE 36 - PATRIOTIC AND NATIONAL OBSERVANCES, CEREMONIES, AND ORGANIZATIONS
- TITLE 37 - PAY AND ALLOWANCES OF THE UNIFORMED SERVICES
- TITLE 38 - VETERANS BENEFITS
- TITLE 39 - POSTAL SERVICE
- TITLE 40 - PUBLIC BUILDINGS, PROPERTY, AND WORKS
- TITLE 41 - PUBLIC CONTRACTS
- TITLE 42 - THE PUBLIC HEALTH AND WELFARE
- TITLE 43 - PUBLIC LANDS
- TITLE 44 - PUBLIC PRINTING AND DOCUMENTS
- TITLE 45 - RAILROADS
- TITLE 46 - SHIPPING
- TITLE 47 - TELEGRAPHS, TELEPHONES, AND RADIOTELEGRAPHS
- TITLE 48 - TERRITORIES AND INSULAR POSSESSIONS
- TITLE 49 - TRANSPORTATION
- TITLE 50 - WAR AND NATIONAL DEFENSE
- TITLE 51 - NATIONAL AND COMMERCIAL SPACE PROGRAMS

So, when a session law is codified, it means that the session law is teased apart and its individual sections are inserted into the code by subject area. An office in Congress called the Office of the Law Revision Counsel takes the session laws and integrates them into the code. For example, the INA was passed in 1952. It was codified in the U.S.C. beginning at section 1101 of title 8. Section 101 of the INA is therefore the same as section 1101 of the U.S.C. Between 1952 and today there have been many changes to the language in section 1101 of the code. The U.S.C. reflects all of those changes. If you want to see the law as it read when it was first introduced in 1952, you would look at section 101 of the 1952 Act. If you want to see the law as it reads today you would look at the 8 U.S.C. § 1101.

Amendments to a particular section are found in the "Credits" immediately following the statutory text. The credits for § 1101 are shown at the top of the next page. You see that it was first introduced in 1952 and then amended in 1980, 1990, 1994, 1996, 2001, 2002, 2005, 2006, and most recently in 2008.

(June 27, 1952, c. 477, Title II, ch. 1, § 208, as added Mar. 17, 1980, Pub.L. 96-212, Title II, § 201(b), 94 Stat. 105; amended Nov. 29, 1990, Pub.L. 101-649, Title V, § 515(a)(1), 104 Stat. 5053; Sept. 13, 1994, Pub.L. 103-322, Title XIII, § 130005(b), 108 Stat. 2028; Apr. 24, 1996, Pub.L. 104-132, Title IV, § 421(a), 110 Stat. 1270; Sept. 30, 1996, Pub.L. 104-208, Div. C, Title VI, § 604(a), 110 Stat. 3009-690; Oct. 26, 2001, Pub.L. 107-56, Title IV, § 411(b)(2), 115 Stat. 348; Aug. 6, 2002, Pub.L. 107-208, § 4, 116 Stat. 928; May 11, 2005, Pub.L. 109-13, Div. B, Title I, § 101(a), (b), 119 Stat. 302, 303; May 8, 2008, Pub.L. 110-229, Title VII, § 702(j) (4), 122 Stat. 866; Dec. 23, 2008, Pub.L. 110-457, Title II, § 235(d)(7), 122 Stat. 5080.)   Most recent amendment

A session law may have sections codified in many different titles of the code. The subject-organized United States Code is therefore a far more research-friendly product than the chronologically-organized United States Statutes at Large. As does the organization of the U.S.C. in general, the organization of each title lends itself to successful legal research as neighboring statutory sections generally involve the same subject area and are likely part of the same statutory framework.

*   *   *

Publication of the U.S.C. and Statutory Citation

The United States Code is officially republished every six years. In the interim period the U.S.C. is updated with supplements. The most recent publication of the U.S.C. was in 2006; the 2012 edition should be published shortly. When citing to the U.S.C., you need to include the code as published in 2006 **and** note the year of any supplement that includes amending language. An example of such a citation is **26 U.S.C. § 302 (2006 & Supp. V 2011)**, which shows that section 302 of title 26 was in existence in 2006 and then amended in 2011. For more information on citing to statutes, see *The Law Student's* Quick Guide *to Legal Citation* (2d ed. 2013).

UNITED STATES CODE

2006 EDITION

CONTAINING THE GENERAL AND PERMANENT LAWS
OF THE UNITED STATES ENACTED THROUGH THE
109TH CONGRESS

(ending January 3, 2007, the last law of which was signed on January 15, 2007)

Prepared and published under authority of Title 2, U.S. Code, Section 285b,
by the Office of the Law Revision Counsel of the House of Representatives

Parts of a Statute
(in this case, a code section, 2 U.S.C. § 202)

Section Number

Section Name

Text of Statute

§ 202. Preparation and publication of Codes and Supplements

There shall be prepared and published under the supervision of the Committee on the Judiciary of the House of Representatives—

(a) Cumulative Supplements to Code of Laws of United States for each session of Congress.— A supplement for each session of the Congress to the then current edition of the Code of Laws of the United States, cumulatively embracing the legislation of the then current supplement, and correcting errors in such edition and supplement;

(b) Cumulative Supplement to District of Columbia Code for each session of Congress.—A supplement for each session of the Congress to the then current edition of the Code of the District of Columbia, cumulatively embracing the legislation of the then current supplement, and correcting errors in such edition and supplement;

(c) New editions of Codes and Supplements.— New editions of the Code of Laws of the United States and of the Code of the District of Columbia, correcting errors and incorporating the then current supplement. In the case of each code new editions shall not be published oftener than once in each five years. Copies of each such edition shall be distributed in the same manner as provided in the case of supplements to the code of which it is a new edition. Supplements published after any new edition shall not contain the legislation of supplements published before such new edition.

(July 30, 1947, ch. 388, 61 Stat. 637.)

CROSS REFERENCES

Cross References

Council of the District of Columbia, functions respecting, see section 2 of Pub. L. 94–386, Aug. 14, 1976, 90 Stat. 1170, set out as a note under section 285b of Title 2, The Congress.

Office of the Law Revision Counsel, functions respecting preparation, revision, publication, etc., see section 285b of Title 2.

Enactment and amendment information. This means that this particular statute was enacted on July 30, 1947 as part of the 388th law passed in that particular session of Congress [Under the numbering system used from 1789 until 1957, the acts passed in each session were numbered sequentially as chapters] and that the law is published in its original form (prior to codification) at page 637 of volume 61 of the United States Statutes at Large.

*   *   *

State Session Laws

States have a very similar legal publication structure to the federal system described above. Their legislatures all meet in sessions, the timing of which varies from state to state. For example, the Texas legislature meets only every two years.

In these sessions, the legislators pass laws that are sometimes referred to as session laws, but labels can vary from state to state. In Massachusetts, for example, session laws are called Chapters, and in Connecticut they are called Public Acts. Irrespective of what they are called, session laws in all states are codified following passage, which means they are placed into the state code. The purpose of codification on the state level is the same as on the federal level, to give citizens a place to look where they can see the current language of a law incorporating all amendments.

* * *

State Codes

A state code is a current snapshot of the law in a particular state. State codes are structured in various ways, and here are a few examples:

> ALA. CODE § 30-2-1 (2011)
> CAL. FAMILY CODE § 2310 (WEST 2004)
> 750 ILL. COMP. STAT. 5/401 (1999)

The Alabama Code citation strings together the title, Title 30 – Marital & Domestic Relations – the chapter, Chapter 2 – Divorce & Alimony – and the article, Article 1 – Divorce from Bonds of Matrimony. The California Code is actually a compilation of many different codes, all of which have their own name. So the California Family Code has individual sections and Sec. 2310 is Grounds for Dissolution or Legal Separation. The Illinois Code has different titles. The citation above shows Title 750 – Families – an act number, Act 5 – Marriage and Dissolution of Marriage Act - and a section number, sec. 401 – Dissolution of Marriage. Every state code is organized differently and doing research in an unfamiliar state requires becoming familiar with the structure of the code in that state.

* * *

Publication of State Codes and Statutory Citation

Many state codes are not published by the state itself as an official set, so citation is to the set recommended in *The Bluebook* in Table 1. Every set of statutes is published on a different schedule, sometimes with different volumes being republished in different years. The theory of citation to a statutory code is the same as discussed with the U.S.C above: cite to the publication date of the volume in which the language of the statutory section appears **and** to the pocket part, but only if there are substantive changes found in the pocket part.

*   *   *

Beginning Statutory Research

How do you find statutes? Should you look up "Clean Water Act," or 33 U.S.C. § 1251, or just start reading Title 33 until you find what you are looking for? What if you are looking for something less obvious than the Clean Water Act; like whether federal law prohibits sending alcohol through the mail?

There are many ways to find statutes, including by Citation, using a Popular Name Table, using a subject index, browsing the table of contents, or doing a keyword search. Your search method will vary depending on whether you're using print or online resources. If you're researching online, not all platforms will have the same features. Federal statutes are available in a variety of locations, including from federal government websites and from paid providers, such as LexisNexis, Westlaw, and Bloomberg Law. The paid versions tend to be more searchable than those found on government websites, but if you just need the text of the statute, the free versions can work just as well.

Generally, we recommend against keyword searching when researching statutes. While keyword searching can at times be successful, for the novice researcher, it can also be confusing. This is because the aim of statutory research is often the answer to a very specific question like, for example, what damages are available to a plaintiff in an employment discrimination lawsuit. The answer to the question will often be found in one specific statutory section only. Because a search produces a list of results that must necessarily be analyzed and the correct result may not be listed on the first page (or perhaps at all), it is often better to research statutes using topical research tools like indexes and tables of contents, which offer more precision than a keyword search.

*   *   *

Annotated v. Unannotated Codes

The United States Code comes in three versions, one official and two unofficial. The first is simply called the U.S.C., and it is the official *unannotated* version of the code. Westlaw and LexisNexis publish unofficial *annotated* versions of the code called, respectively, the United States Code Annotated (U.S.C.A.) and the United States Code Service (U.S.C.S.). When researching statutes, you should always use an *annotated* code. Annotated codes provide you with not only the text of the statute, but also related cases and secondary sources that interpret the statute and help you see how it may be applied in a situation that is factually similar to yours. This is vital as statutes may be framed in ambiguous language that is often difficult to interpret.

The annotations consist of brief summaries of cases organized by subject that are designed to provide enough information to determine the case's relevance and value. The case annotations, called Notes of Decisions, from 10 U.S.C.A. § 1212 are shown below.

Ch. 61 PHYSICAL DISABILITY   **10 § 1212**

LIBRARY REFERENCES

American Digest System
    Armed Services ☞5(3), 5(6), 13.5(5), 23.4(3).
    Key Number System Topic No. 34.

Notes of Decisions

Recall to active duty 1
Reinstatement 2
Weight and sufficiency of evidence 3

---

1. Recall to active duty

  Where the military or naval service recalls to active duty in a limited service capacity an officer who should have been but was not retired for physical disability upon findings of service incurred permanent incapacity approved by the Secretary, such recall will not deprive the officer of the benefits otherwise resulting from the determination of his permanent incapacity, approved by the Secretary. Lerner v. U.S., Ct.Cl.1964, 168 Ct.Cl. 247. Armed Services ☞ 13.5(10)

  Where the Navy recalls to active duty in wartime a man who has been retired for physical disability, and the Chief of Naval Personnel directs the man's commanding officer to comply with the opinion of the Bureau of Medicine and Surgery with respect to the assignment of responsibilities to the man, i.e., to shore duty not involving prolonged or strenuous physical exertion, it is clear that the purpose of the recall was to release able-bodied men for more demanding duties or combat and was not to countermand or change the character of the recalled man's disability retirement. Akol v. U.S., Ct.Cl.1964, 167 Ct.Cl. 99. Armed Services ☞ 23.4(3)

2. Reinstatement

  Where the Army had improperly discharged plaintiff sergeant as permanently unfit for duty the sergeant, who prior to the permanent discharge had been placed on temporary disability retired list because of alleged schizophrenic reaction, was entitled to reinstatement for a period at least equivalent to the time which remained on his enlistment contract when he was placed on the temporary list; sergeant was to be reenlisted, with his consent, at rank he held at time he was placed on the temporary list, subject to discretion of Secretary of the Army to reenlist him in the next higher grade. Craft v. U.S., Ct.Cl.1976, 544 F.2d 468, 210 Ct.Cl. 170. Armed Services ☞ 22(7)

  Army Board for Correction of Military Records did not act arbitrarily and capriciously by denying reinstatement to active duty after determination of service member's physical fitness and removal of service member from temporary disability retired list; Board considered member's poor military evaluations prior to establishment of emotional problems; and medical records and military evaluations showed instability and personal inadequacy. Pope v. U.S., Cl.Ct.1989, 16 Cl. Ct. 637. Armed Services ☞ 11(6)

3. Weight and sufficiency of evidence

  Denying further disability retirement pay to Army captain, a doctor, who suffered from ulcer condition, on ground that he was physically fit for active duty was so contrary to compelling weight of evidence that it could not be sustained. Versaci v. U.S., Ct.Cl.1968, 403 F.2d 246, 185 Ct.Cl. 672. Armed Services ☞ 13.5(5.2)

Search Methods

Finding a Statute by Citation

The easiest way to find a statute is by code citation.

Finding a Code Citation in Print

As discussed previously, the U.S.C. is organized by title, and further broken down by parts, chapters, subchapters, and sections. Parts, chapters, and subchapters are primarily used for organizational purposes within the code itself, and do not appear in citations, unlike the title and section numbers, which do. A complete citation to a U.S.C. section looks like this.

42 U.S.C. § 1983 (2006).

42 is the number of the title, which corresponds to the subject area *Public Health and Welfare*, and **1983** is the section number within title 42. As noted, neighboring sections cover the same subject area or may be part of the same statutory framework. The best way to see these relationships is to look at a table of contents. A part of the table of contents for the statutory framework containing section 1983 is below.

CHAPTER 21—CIVIL RIGHTS
SUBCHAPTER I—GENERALLY

Sec.	
1981.	Equal rights under the law.
1981a.	Damages in cases of intentional discrimination in employment.
1982.	Property rights of citizens.
1983.	Civil action for deprivation of rights.
1984.	Omitted.
1985.	Conspiracy to interfere with civil rights.
1986.	Action for neglect to prevent.
1987.	Prosecution of violation of certain laws.
1988.	Proceedings in vindication of civil rights.
1989.	United States magistrate judges; appointment of persons to execute warrants.
1990.	Marshal to obey precepts; refusing to receive or execute process.
1991.	Fees; persons appointed to execute process.
1992.	Speedy trial.
1993.	Repealed.
1994.	Peonage abolished.
1995.	Criminal contempt proceedings; penalties; trial by jury.
1996.	Protection and preservation of traditional religions of Native Americans.
1996a.	Traditional Indian religious use of peyote.
1996b.	Interethnic adoption.

When researching statutes, it is important to analyze the code in groups of statutory sections. For example, while section 1983 outlines the availability of a civil action against a public official for the deprivation of rights, section 1981a outlines the damages available in such an action, section 1988 outlines the nature of the proceedings to vindicate those rights, etc. In other words, one statutory section seldom provides the entire answer. Analysis of the complete statutory framework is nearly always necessary.

If you are looking up a statute by citation in the print volumes of the U.S.C., the first step is to locate the volume that contains the relevant title. Some titles of the U.S.C. are very large, and are contained in more than one volume, so make sure you get the correct volume.

As you can see from scanning the spines of the books (a very effective research method in and of itself), many volumes contain parts of title 42, but only one has the section we want. Once you have located the correct volume (here, we want volume 25), flip to your section. You can see section 1983 on the next page. Please note again the various parts of the statute; in particular, the historical, codification, and amendment information.

The statutory credits are very important. They show that § 1983 was originally passed in 1871 as part of the legislation designed to enforce the 14th Amendment. It was originally codified in the Revised Statutes (the precursor to the U.S.C.) at § 1979. It was amended in 1979 by Pub. L. No. 96-170 and again in 1996 by Pub. L. No. 104-317.

§ 1983. Civil action for deprivation of rights

Every person who, under color of any statute, ordinance, regulation, custom, or usage, of any State or Territory or the District of Columbia, subjects, or causes to be subjected, any citizen of the United States or other person within the jurisdiction thereof to the deprivation of any rights, privileges, or immunities secured by the Constitution and laws, shall be liable to the party injured in an action at law, suit in equity, or other proper proceeding for redress, except that in any action brought against a judicial officer for an act or omission taken in such officer's judicial capacity, injunctive relief shall not be granted unless a declaratory decree was violated or declaratory relief was unavailable. For the purposes of this section, any Act of Congress applicable exclusively to the District of Columbia shall be considered to be a statute of the District of Columbia.

(R.S. § 1979; Pub. L. 96-170, § 1, Dec. 29, 1979, 93 Stat. 1284; Pub. L. 104-317, title III, § 309(c), Oct. 19, 1996, 110 Stat. 3853.)

CODIFICATION

R.S. § 1979 derived from act Apr. 20, 1871, ch. 22, § 1, 17 Stat. 13.

Section was formerly classified to section 43 of Title 8, Aliens and Nationality.

AMENDMENTS

1996—Pub. L. 104-317 inserted before period at end of first sentence ", except that in any action brought against a judicial officer for an act or omission taken in such officer's judicial capacity, injunctive relief shall not be granted unless a declaratory decree was violated or declaratory relief was unavailable".

1979—Pub. L. 96-170 inserted "or the District of Columbia" after "Territory", and provisions relating to Acts of Congress applicable solely to the District of Columbia.

Finding a Citation Online

Many online databases permit searches for statutory sections by citation. For example, on the Office of Law Revision Counsel's ("OLRC") U.S. Code Beta site [**http://uscode.house.gov/beta.shtml**],[14] typing in the correct title and section number will retrieve any provision of the U.S.C. you choose (for free!).

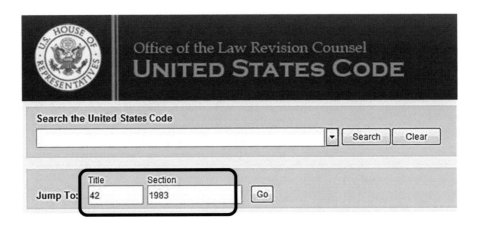

The result is below. Please note again the various parts of the statute.

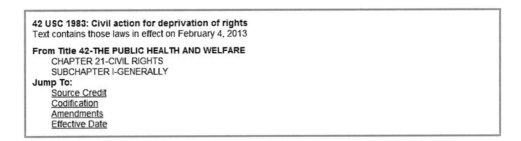

§1983. Civil action for deprivation of rights

   Every person who, under color of any statute, ordinance, regulation, custom, or usage, of any State or Territory or the District of Columbia, subjects, or causes to be subjected, any citizen of the United States or other person within the jurisdiction thereof to the deprivation of any rights, privileges, or immunities secured by the Constitution and laws, shall be liable to the party injured in an action at law, suit in equity, or other proper proceeding for redress, except that in any action brought against a judicial officer for an act or omission taken in such officer's judicial capacity, injunctive relief shall not be granted unless a declaratory decree was violated or declaratory relief was unavailable. For the purposes of this section, any Act of Congress applicable exclusively to the District of Columbia shall be considered to be a statute of the District of Columbia.

(R.S. §1979; Pub. L. 96–170, §1, Dec. 29, 1979, 93 Stat. 1284; Pub. L. 104–317, title III, §309(c), Oct. 19, 1996, 110 Stat. 3853.)

You can also find a code section using Google by typing in the full citation.

---

[14]   Pursuant to 2 U.S.C. § 285b, the Office of the Law Revision Counsel, an office of the United States House of Representatives, prepares and publishes the official version of the United States Code.

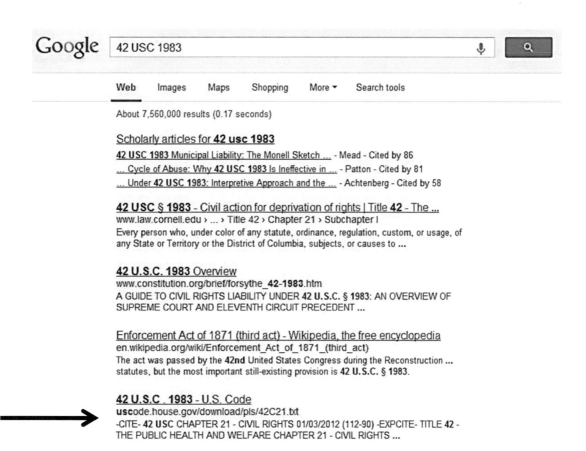

Google locates the statute and also returns several results that mention the statute, but don't actually provide the statutory text, so you have to examine the results carefully before choosing one. While Google is good for many things, if you are looking specifically for a federal statute, you are better off choosing the Office of Law Revision Council's U.S. Code Beta site (noted above) or the U.S. Code Collection from the Government Printing Office's Federal Digital System ("GPO FDSys") at **http://www.gpo.gov/fdsys**. That way you know you are accessing the accurate, official version of the U.S.C.

In Lexis Advance and WestlawNext, type your citation into the search bar on the home screen to find the statutory text.

*　　*　　*

Finding a Statute by Popular Name

If your statute has a popular name, like the Clean Water Act or the Family and Medical Leave Act, you can look it up in a Popular Names Table (Sometimes known as a Short Title Index in some state statute compilations). A Popular Names Table is an alphabetical listing of statutes by popular or statutory name. For federal statutes, each popular name entry lists the name of the statute, the public law number, the Statutes at Large citation, and the location in the U.S.C. where the statute has been codified.

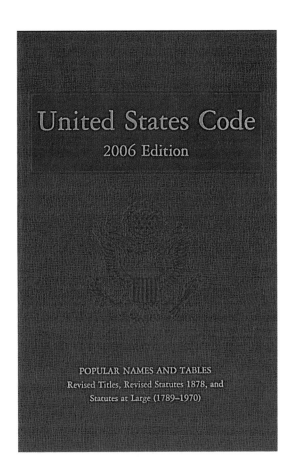

United States Code
2006 Edition

POPULAR NAMES AND TABLES
Revised Titles, Revised Statutes 1878, and
Statutes at Large (1789–1970)

To find the Clean Water Act in the United States Code using the Popular Name Table in print, go to the section of the Popular Name Table that starts with "C" and browse through alphabetically to find the entry for the Clean Water Act. As you can see below, the Clean Water Act was Public Law 95-217, and it can be found in the Statutes at Large at 91 Stat. 1566. It was codified in the U.S.C. starting at 33 U.S.C. § 1251.

ACTS CITED BY POPULAR NAME   Page 40

Class Action Fairness Act of 2005
    Pub. L. 109–2, Feb. 18, 2005, 119 Stat.
    Short title, see 28 U.S.C. 1 note

Classification Act Amendments of 1962
    Pub. L. 87–793, part II, title II, Oct. 11, 1962,
    76 Stat. 843

Classification Act of 1923
    Mar. 4, 1923, ch. 265, 42 Stat. 1488

Classification Act of 1949
    Oct. 28, 1949, ch. 782, 63 Stat. 954

Classified Information Procedures Act
    Pub. L. 96–456, Oct. 15, 1980, 94 Stat. 2025 (18
    U.S.C. App.)
    Short title, see 18 U.S.C. App. 16

Clean Water Act of 1977
    Pub. L. 95–217, Dec. 27, 1977, 91 Stat. 1566
    Short title, see 33 U.S.C. 1251 note

Clean Water for the America Partnership Act of 2002
    Pub. L. 107–228, div. A, title VI, subtitle D
    (§ 641 et seq.), Sept. 30, 2002, 116 Stat. 1402
    (22 U.S.C. 2151p note)

Clean Water Restoration Act of 1966
    Pub. L. 89–753, Nov. 3, 1966, 80 Stat. 1246

Clear Creek County, Colorado, Public Lands Transfer Act of 1993
    Pub. L. 103–253, May 19, 1994, 108 Stat. 674

Clear Creek Distribution System Conveyance Act
    Pub. L. 106–566, title IV, Dec. 23, 2000, 114

An advantage to using the Popular Name Table is that if the name you look up is not the one most commonly used, you will be redirected to the correct entry. For example, the more common name for the Air Pollution Control Act is the Clean Air Act. When you look up Air Pollution Control Act in the Popular Name Table, you are redirected to the correct entry.

Air Mail Act
    Feb. 2, 1925, ch. 128, 43 Stat. 805

Air Pollution Control Act
    See Clean Air Act

Air Quality Act of 1967
    Pub. L. 90–148, Nov. 21, 1967, 81 Stat. 485
    Short title, see 42 U.S.C. 7401 note

Air Raid Attack Act
    Jan. 27, 1942, ch. 20, 56 Stat. 19

Airport and Airway Development Act Amendments of 1976
    Pub. L. 94–353, July 12, 1976, 90 Stat. 871

Airport and Airway Development Act of 1970
    Pub. L. 91–258, title I, May 21, 1970, 84 Stat. 219

Airport and Airway Extension Act of 2008
    Pub. L. 110–190, Feb. 28, 2008, 122 Stat. 643
    Short title, see 26 U.S.C. 1 note

Airport and Airway Extension Act of 2010

When you turn to the Clean Air Act, you are then given the Public Law number, Statutes at Large citation, and the location in the U.S.C. Below the entry for the Clean Air Act, you can also see the entries for subsequent amendments.

Clayton Act (Antitrust)
Oct. 15, 1914, ch. 323, 38 Stat. 730 (15 U.S.C. 12 et seq.)
Short title, see 15 U.S.C. 12(b)

Clean Air Act
July 14, 1955, ch. 360, 69 Stat. 322 (42 U.S.C. 7401 et seq.)
Short title, see 42 U.S.C. 7401 note

Clean Air Act Amendments of 1966
Pub. L. 89–675, Oct. 15, 1966, 80 Stat. 954
Short title, see 42 U.S.C. 7401 note

Clean Air Act Amendments of 1977
Pub. L. 95–95, Aug. 7, 1977, 91 Stat. 685
Short title, see 42 U.S.C. 7401 note

Clean Air Act Amendments of 1990
Pub. L. 101–549, Nov. 15, 1990, 104 Stat. 2399
Short title, see 42 U.S.C. 7401 note

Clean Air Amendments of 1970
Pub. L. 91–604, Dec. 31, 1970, 84 Stat. 1676
Short title, see 42 U.S.C. 7401 note

Short title, see 26 U.S.C. 1 note
Clinger-Cohen Act of 1996
Pub. L. 104–106, divs. D, E, Feb. 10, 1996, 110 Stat. 642, 679
Short title, see 41 U.S.C. 101 note

Clinical Laboratories Improvement Act of 1967
Pub. L. 90–174, §5, Dec. 5, 1967, 81 Stat. 536 (42 U.S.C. 263a)
Short title, see 42 U.S.C. 201 note

Clinical Laboratory Improvement Amendments of 1988
Pub. L. 100–578, Oct. 31, 1988, 102 Stat. 2903
Short title, see 42 U.S.C. 201 note

Clinical Research Enhancement Act of 2000
Pub. L. 106–505, title II, Nov. 13, 2000, 114 Stat. 2325
Short title, see 42 U.S.C. 201 note

Close the Contractor Fraud Loophole Act
Pub. L. 110–252, title VI, chapter 1 (§6101 et seq.), June 30, 2008, 122 Stat. 2386 (41 U.S.C. 101 note)

Using the Popular Name Table Online

At the OLRC's U.S.C. Popular Names Tool, use the hyperlinked menu on the right to jump to the section of the tool that lists acts by popular name for that letter of the alphabet.

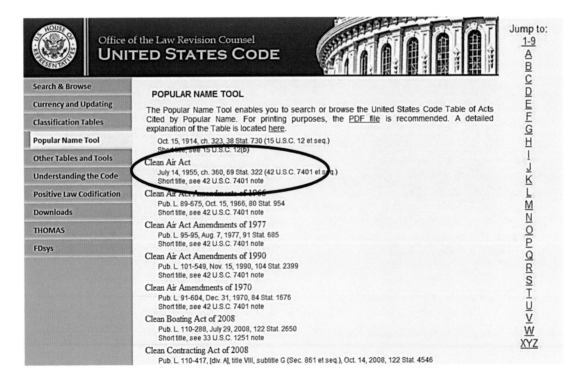

On WestlawNext, to access the Popular Name Table, begin typing "USCA Popular Name Table" into the search box and select it from the drop-down menu that appears.

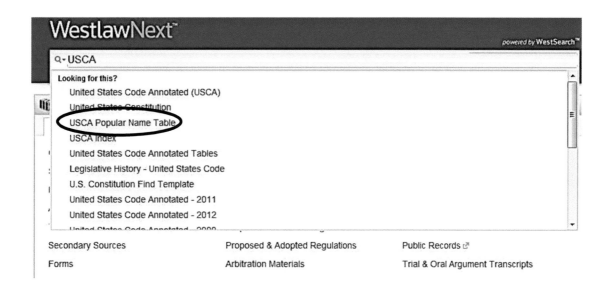

Use the alphabet at the top of the screen to navigate to your section of the Popular Name Table. Then, scroll through the listings to find your act.

One of the benefits of using the Popular Name Table on Westlaw is that selecting the statute in which you are interested brings up a table showing how the sections of the session law correspond with those of the U.S.C. An example using the Clean Air Act is below. The original sections of the Clean Air Act session law are on the left. The corresponding U.S.C. sections are on the right.

Clean Air Act (Air Pollution Control Act) (CAA)
July 14, 1955, ch. 360, 69 Stat. 322
Short title, see 42 USCA § 7401 note

Current USCA classifications:

Section of ch. 360	USCA Classification
101	42 USCA § 7401
102	42 USCA § 7402
103	42 USCA § 7403
104	42 USCA § 7404
105	42 USCA § 7405
106	42 USCA § 7406
107	42 USCA § 7407
108	42 USCA § 7408
109	42 USCA § 7409
110	42 USCA § 7410
111	42 USCA § 7411

Lexis Advance does not have a Popular Name Table. The best way to find an act by name in Lexis Advance is to type the name into the search box, open the first case that contains your search term, and use the hyperlink to access the statute. Note that this will not give you the Public Law Number or Statutes at Large citation like you see in other tools.

*   *   *

Finding a Statute Using the Subject Index

What if the statute you are looking for doesn't have a popular name? Or, what if you are not looking for a specific session law, but rather you are looking to see what laws exist on a particular topic? For example, what if you had been asked to give a presentation to a group of undergraduates on what law school is like, and you wanted to use clips from movies like *The Paper Chase* and *Legally Blonde*, but weren't sure if it was acceptable to show them to an audience without a license? You could use a Subject Index to look up terms relating to your research question and find the applicable statutes. As noted previously, this is often a better method than keyword searching for statutes as the index can lead you directly to the statutory section in which you are interested.

Subject indexes are primarily found in print materials. Some online resources, however, will also have a subject index, such as the United States Code Annotated, which is found on Westlaw. One advantage of using a subject index is that, similar to the Popular Names Table, the index will help redirect you to an appropriate term if you are off the mark at first. As with searching, to use the subject index, it helps to have used the four-step research method and to have collected key terms related to your legal issue before beginning.

Using the Subject Index in Print

By way of another example, suppose you are continuing your research into the law related to clean water, and are now expanding that research to examine issues related to invasive aquatic species, like for example, zebra mussels. Using the U.S.C.'s print General Index, first turn to the "I" section and look for "invasive species" (you also, of course, could just start with "zebra mussels," but for the sake of the exercise and to show how the index works, let's start with our broadest term).

INTRASTATE PIPELINE
Natural Gas, this index

INTRAVENOUS DRUG ABUSERS
Drug Addicts, generally, this index

INTRAVENOUS IMMUNE GLOBULIN
Medicare, 42 §§ 1395l, 1395x

INUITS
Eskimos, generally, this index

INVASION OF PRIVACY
Right of Privacy, generally, this index

INVEIGLE AND INVEIGLING
Kidnapping, generally, this index

A subject index is organized alphabetically by key words (in bold) and more specific subheadings.

But "Invasive Species" is not included in the index. This is where having a list of search terms comes in handy. Now, skip to the next term on your list, "mussels." (You see where this is going, I'm sure).

MUSIC—Continued

Surveys, 36 §152301 et seq.
Taxation, exemptions, National Federation of Music Clubs, 36 §151508

MUSKINGUM WATERSHED CONSERVANCY DISTRICT

Floods and flood control, 33 §701c–1

MUSKOGEE, OK

National banks, reserve city, 12 §141

MUSLIM COUNTRIES

Culture, exchange, 22 §2451 note
Education, exchange, 22 §2451 note
Foreign Service, foreign languages, 22 §3922b
International Youth Opportunity Fund, 22 §2228
Mutual educational and cultural exchange, 22 §2451 note
Schools and school districts, American-sponsored schools, grants, 22 §2452 note
United States international broadcasting, 22 §1451 note

MUSSELS

Aquaculture, generally, this index
Endangered Species, generally, this index
Mississippi River, propagation, 16 §750
Zebra Mussels, generally, this index

High seas, 18 §§2192, 2193
Military Justice Code, this index
Military offenses, 18 §§2387, 2388
National service life insurance, fines, penalties and forfeitures, 38 §1911
Seamen, 18 §§2192, 2193
Servicemembers group life insurance, fines, penalties and forfeitures, 38 §1973
Veterans, this index

MUTUAL AID AGREEMENTS

National capital region, 42 §5196 note

MUTUAL BANK HOLDING COMPANY

Bank Holding Company, this index

MUTUAL COMPANIES

Fair housing, 42 §3601 et seq.

MUTUAL COOPERATIVE BANKS

Cooperative Banks, generally, this index

MUTUAL EDUCATIONAL AND CULTURAL EXCHANGE

Generally, 22 §2451 et seq.
Acquisitions, foreign currency, 22 §2455
Administration, 22 §§2454, 2454 note, Ex. Ord. No. 11034
Administrative expenses, Bureau of Educational

Here, the subject index redirects you to the proper term, which is Zebra Mussels.

YUGOSLAVIA—Continued

Refugees, Kosovo, 8 §1157 note
Rewards, human rights violations, 22 §2708 note
Serbia and Montenegro,
  Assistance, restrictions, waiver, 50 §1701 note
  Combat zones, income tax, 26 §112 note, Ex. Ord. No. 13119
  Income tax, combat zones, 26 §112 note, Ex. Ord. No. 13119
  International trade, withdrawal of trade, 19 §2434 note
  National emergency, 50 §1701 note, Ex. Ord. No. 12808; 50 §1701 note
  Restrictions, assistance, waiver, 50 §1701 note
  Sanctions, 50 §1701 note
  Waiver, restrictions, assistance, 50 §1701 note
  Withdrawal of trade, 19 §2434 note
United States person, definitions, national emergency, 50 §1701 note, Ex. Ord. No. 12808
War claims, 50 App. §2017 et seq.
War crimes, genocide, 22 §2656 note

YUKON–CHARLEY NATIONAL MONUMENT

Generally, 16 §431 note

YWCA

Young Women's Christian Association, generally, this index

ZAIRE

Foreign assistance, 22 §2370 note
International trade, Generalized System of Preferences, 19 §2462 note, Proc. No. 6942

ZAMBIA

Copyrights, 17 §104 note
International trade, Generalized System of Preferences, 19 §2462 note, Proc. No. 6942

ZEBRA MUSSELS

Appropriations, research, 33 §1131
Crimes and offenses, exports and imports, 18 §42
Exports and imports, crimes and offenses, 18 §42
Lake Champlain, 16 §4701
Research, appropriations, 33 §1131
States, managers and management, plans and specifications, 16 §4724

ZIMBABWE DEMOCRACY AND ECONOMIC RECOVERY ACT OF

Under the term "Zebra Mussels," you see a list of all the statutes in the U.S.C. that relate to Zebra Mussels.

Using the Subject Index Online

Lexis Advance, GPO FDSys, and the OLRC's U.S. Code site do not have subject indexes for the U.S.C. The only online tool with an index is WestlawNext.

To access the index on WestlawNext, type "USCA Index" into the search box.

Use the hyperlinked alphabet at the top of the page to access the section of the index that contains your search term.

Click the hyperlink to view the U.S. Code sections related to your search term.

Zebra Mussels 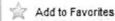 Add to Favorites

Appropriations, Research: 33 USCA § 1131

Crimes and Offenses, Exports and Imports: 18 USCA § 42

Exports and Imports, Crimes and Offenses: 18 USCA § 42

Lake Champlain: 16 USCA § 4701

Research, Appropriations: 33 USCA § 1131

States, Managers and Management, Plans and Specifications: 16 USCA § 4724

Then, click the hyperlinks to view the individual code sections.

See the difference between searching using an index and searching by keyword? The index provides an exact, topic-centered result. The keyword search, which examines the terms in the statutory sections and does not search by topic, does not. Indeed, a keyword search for statutes may not provide any helpful results as the words in the text of the statute may not be the words that you are using to search.

*   *   *

Finding Statutes Using a Table of Contents

Whether or not you have a particular code provision in mind, the table of contents can be a good way to expand or perhaps even begin your research.

Using a Table of Contents in Print

The print United States Code has a Table of Contents at the beginning of each volume, which details the contents of each title of the code.

TABLE OF TITLES AND CHAPTERS

There is also a shorter table of contents for the volume itself.

CONTENTS

For each title.

TITLE 28—JUDICIARY AND JUDICIAL PROCEDURE

This title was enacted by act June 25, 1948, ch. 646, § 1, 62 Stat. 869

For each part within a title.

PART I—ORGANIZATION OF COURTS

And for each chapter within a part, which finally reveals the individual statutory sections.

CHAPTER 85—DISTRICT COURTS; JURISDICTION

To find a statute by browsing the table of contents, examine the titles of the code (you can do this by looking at the spines of the books, which is almost always a good idea anyway) until you find one that looks relevant. Then browse the more detailed tables of contents within that title until you find the section that looks relevant. Browsing a table of contents is most effective when you already have a title or statute to start with. As noted, browsing can help you find related statutes and help put your section in context by identifying neighboring statutory sections. When researching statutes, you should always browse the table of contents at some point, even if it's not your primary research method.

Using the Table of Contents Online

Online sources are also structured so you can browse the code based on the table of contents. For example, if you look at the U.S.C. on GPO FDSys, you can browse all the titles. You can also expand each title to see the chapters and sections contained within that title.

⊞ Title 1 – GENERAL PROVISIONS
Sections 1 – 213.

⊞ Title 2 – THE CONGRESS
Sections 1 – 2281.

⊞ Title 3 – THE PRESIDENT
Sections 1 – 471.

⊞ Title 4 – FLAG AND SEAL, SEAT OF GOVERNMENT, AND THE STATES
Sections 1 – 146.

⊞ Title 5 – GOVERNMENT ORGANIZATION AND EMPLOYEES
Sections 101 – 10210.

⊞ Title 6 – DOMESTIC SECURITY
Sections 101 – 1405.

⊟ Title 7 – AGRICULTURE
Sections 1 – 8922.

    Table Of Contents

    ⊟ CHAPTER 1 – COMMODITY EXCHANGES (sections 1 – 27f)

        Table Of Contents

        Sec. 1 – Short title

        Sec. 1a – Definitions

        Sec. 1b – Requirements of Secretary of the Treasury regarding exemption of foreign exchange swaps and...

        Sec. 2 – Jurisdiction of Commission; liability of principal for act of agent; Commodity Futures Trading...

        Secs. 2a to 4a – Transferred

        Sec. 5 – Findings and purpose

        Sec. 6 – Regulation of futures trading and foreign transactions

        Sec. 6a – Excessive speculation

        Sec. 6b – Contracts designed to defraud or mislead

Both Lexis Advance and WestlawNext have tables of contents for the U.S.C. as well. They are best used to see individual statutory sections in context.

So, on WestlawNext, when viewing a statutory section, always click on the Table of Contents button to find the statutory framework.

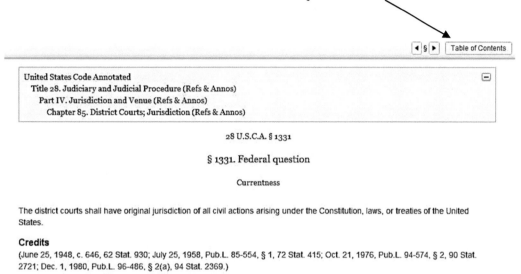

The click reveals the Table of Contents.

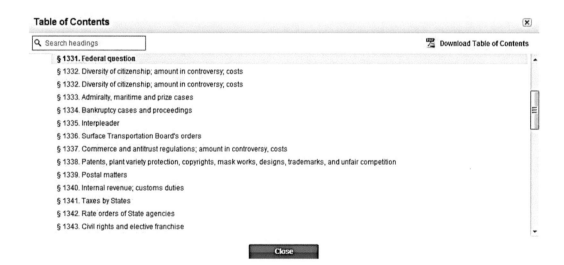

Do the same thing on Lexis Advance.

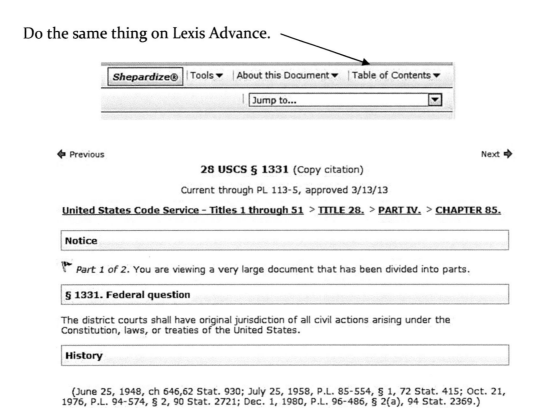

Clicking the link, reveals the table of contents in a drop down menu.

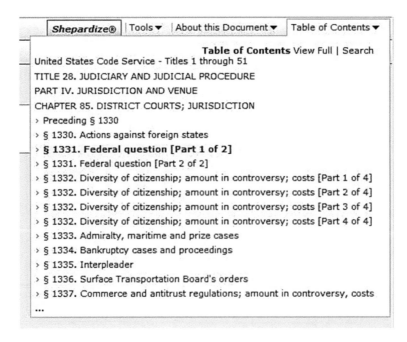

Always use tables of contents when researching statutes. You need to see the statutory section in context. You need to understand the statutory framework.

*　　*　　*

Finding Statutes Using a Keyword Search

Keyword searching is a good method of research to use when you know the topic you're researching, but not the specific statutes in that area. Unlike a subject index, however, you're on your own when it comes to thinking up search terms. If you use a search term that is not used in the statute, applicable statutes may not be retrieved. You can end your research thinking there are no applicable laws on your topic, when in reality, you just missed finding them because you didn't have the right search terms. Keyword searching is a good tool to use after you've done some preliminary research in secondary sources, have a good handle on what the common terms are, and have created a good list of search terms to try. Unlike the other search methods we have looked at, keyword searching can only be done in online resources.

*　　*　　*

Updating

When you research in print, you will need to check to make sure you have the most up-to-date version of the statute.

When using print resources, use the pocket part to update your research. The pocket part is a small paper pamphlet tucked into the back of your main volume or (if it gets too big), a separately bound softcover book on the shelf immediately next to your main volume. The pocket part is organized identically to the main volume. To update your research using the pocket part, look for your code section. If the text of your code section does *not* appear in the pocket part, the statute in the main volume is the most up-to-date version. If the text of your statute is in the pocket part, you will need to read it carefully to determine what has been changed or added, and use the updated version instead.

*　　*　　*

Practice Questions

1.   Find 18 U.S.C. § 1657. What is the title of this section? When was it last amended?

2.   What departmental secretary is authorized to prohibit the importation of honeybees into the US?

3.   In what section of the US Code can you find the findings and declaration of policy of the Mushroom Promotion, Research, and Consumer Information Act of 1990?

4.   May the captain of a ship sailing from the U.S. to France carry a private letter? (i.e., one not sent through the U.S. Mail?)

5.   What provision of the U.S. Code gives Amtrak the right to operate nationwide passenger train service?

6.   7 U.S.C. § 6001 states that what nut must be "high quality, readily available, handled properly, and marketed efficiently to ensure that all consumers have an adequate supply"?

7.   Against what diseases must an immigrant to the U.S. be vaccinated?

8.   When was the Yellowstone National Park Protection Act enacted? What is its Public Law Number? Where does it appear in the Statutes at Large?

9.   Who administers the oath of office to the President of the Senate?

10.   During what hours may the United States Flag be flown on a rainy day?

11.   Using the Popular Name tool on the US Code beta site (http://143.231.180.80/), find the Sarbanes-Oxley Act of 2002. Where in the US Code is it located? What public law number is it? Where in the Statutes at Large can it be found?

12.   What provisions of the U.S. Code lay out the subject and scope of copyright?

13.   16 U.S.C. § 26 prohibits hunting in Yellowstone National Park. Does this section apply to hunting guides or just hunters themselves? (hint: try using an annotated code for this question).

14.   What did Pub. L. 87-443 establish? Where in the US Code has this been codified?

15.   Which Cabinet-level Department or Secretary is responsible for issuing passports?

16.   Are the waters from the Louisiana Purchase considered public highways?

17.   A cybersquatter has registered the domains mittromney4president.com and mittromneyshairisdabomb.com,

intending to resell it to Mitt Romney for an exorbitant amount of money. What section of the United States Code lays out the civil liability provisions for this practice, known as cyberpiracy?

18.   What are the purposes of the National Yoemen Foundation?

19.   In what title of the U.S. Code can you find the National Flood Insurance Program, the Civil Rights Act, and the National School Lunch program?

20.   What is Megan's Law?

Notes

Notes

Answer Key for Researching Statutes Practice Questions

1. Find 18 U.S.C. § 1657. What is the title of this section? When was it last amended?

   Corruption of seamen and confederating with pirates. Last amended Sept. 13, 1994, Pub. L. 103-322.

2. What departmental secretary is authorized to prohibit the importation of honeybees into the US?

   The Secretary of Agriculture. *See* **7 U.S.C. § 281.**

3. In what section of the US Code can you find the findings and declaration of policy of the Mushroom Promotion, Research, and Consumer Information Act of 1990?

   7 U.S.C. § 6101.

4. May the captain of a ship sailing from the U.S. to France carry a private letter? (i.e., one not sent through the U.S. Mail?)

   No—39 U.S.C. § 602.

5. What provision of the U.S. Code gives Amtrak the right to operate nationwide passenger train service?

   49 U.S.C. § 24701.

6. 7 U.S.C. § 6001 states that what nut must be "high quality, readily available, handled properly, and marketed efficiently to ensure that all consumers have an adequate supply"?

   Pecans

7.   Against what diseases must an immigrant to the U.S. be vaccinated?

Mumps, measles, rubella, polio, tetanus and diphtheria toxoids, pertussis, influenza type B and hepatitis B, and any other vaccinations against vaccine-preventable diseases recommended by the Advisory Committee for Immunization Practices. 8 U.S.C. § 1182(a)(1)(A)(ii)

8.   When was the Yellowstone National Park Protection Act enacted? What is its Public Law Number? Where does it appear in the Statutes at Large?

May 7, 1894, ch. 72, 28 Stat. 73.

9.   Who administers the oath of office to the President of the Senate?

Any member of the Senate. 2 U.S.C. § 22.

10.   During what hours may the United States Flag be flown on a rainy day?

Sunrise to sunset, in good weather only, unless an all-weather flag is used, in which case, it may be flown during inclement weather. A flag may be flown after dark with proper illumination. 4 U.S.C. § 6.

11.   Using the Popular Name tool on the US Code beta site (http://143.231.180.80/), find the Sarbanes-Oxley Act of 2002. Where in the US Code is it located? What public law number is it? Where in the Statutes at Large can it be found?

15 U.S.C. §§ 7201-02, 7211-7220, 7231-34, 7241-46, 7261-66, 780-6, 78d-3, 18 U.S.C. §§ 1519-20, 1514A, 1348-50. Pub. L. 107-204, 116 Stat. 745.

12. What provisions of the U.S. Code lay out the subject and scope of copyright?

   17 U.S.C. §§ 101-122.

13. 16 U.S.C. § 26 prohibits hunting in Yellowstone National Park. Does this section apply to hunting guides or just hunters themselves? (hint: try using an annotated code for this question).

   Yes. *See United States v. Sanford*, 547 F.2d 1085 (C.A.9 1976). It does not, however, apply to park personnel to kill or capture wildlife under approved wildlife management plans. *See Greater Yellowstone Coalition v. Babbitt*, 952 F. Supp. 1435 (D. Mont. 1996).

14. What did Pub. L. 87-443 establish? Where in the US Code has this been codified?

   The National Portrait Gallery as a bureau of the Smithsonian Institution. 20 U.S.C. §§ 75a-g.

15. Which Cabinet-level Department or Secretary is responsible for issuing passports?

   The Secretary of State. 22 U.S.C. § 211a.

16. Are the waters from the Louisiana Purchase considered public highways?

   Yes. 33 U.S.C. § 10.

17. A cybersquatter has registered the domains mittromney4president.com and mittromneyshairisdabomb.com, intending to resell it to Mitt Romney for an exorbitant amount of money. What section of the United States Code lays out the civil liability provisions for this practice, known as cyberpiracy?

15 U.S.C. §§ 1114, 1117, 1127.

18. What are the purposes of the National Yoemen Foundation?

The purposes of the corporation are patriotic, historical, and educational and are--

(1) to foster and perpetuate the memory of the service of Yoemen (f) in the United States Naval Reserve Force of the United States Navy during World War I;

(2) to preserve the memories and incidents of their association in World War I by the encouragement of historical research concerning the service of Yoemen (f);

(3) to cherish, maintain, and extend the institutions of American freedom by the promotion of celebrations of all patriotic anniversaries;

(4) to foster true patriotism and love of country; and

(5) to aid in securing for mankind all the blessings of liberty.
36 U.S.C. § 153902.

19. In what title of the U.S. Code can you find the National Flood Insurance Program, the Civil Rights Act, and the National School Lunch program?

Title 42, Public Health & Welfare.

20. What is Megan's Law?

An Act to amend the Violent Crime Control and Law Enforcement Act of 1994 to require the release of relevant information to protect the public from sexually violent offenders. Pub. L. 104-145.

Updating

Updating

Introduction

So far, we have explored tools for researching secondary sources, which explain an area of law, and tools for researching court decisions, legislation, and regulations, which constitute the primary sources of law in any given jurisdiction. But, no matter the sources you research or the tools you employ, you are not done until you have updated your results. By that we mean it is necessary to verify the current status, or legal authority, of each primary source (including cases and statutes) on which your analysis is based or to which you intend to cite in a legal argument. To do this, it is necessary to use one of several updating tools, also known as **citators**.

* * *

Updating Cases

The Law Set Forth in a Case Can Change

Before relying on a proposition in a case found in your research, you need to determine if the proposition is still "good law." But, what does that mean?

Consider a hypothetical case decided in 1990 by a state's intermediate court of appeals. Before relying on that case, you need to consider what may have happened since your case was decided. There are several things that could have happened to render that case no longer good law: negative direct history (in the same case), negative treatment by a later case, or possible non-judicial changes in the law.

In **direct history**, your 1990 appellate court decision could have been appealed to the highest court in the state; if the higher court reversed or otherwise rejected all or part of the opinion, the proposition for which you would like to cite the case may not be good law. *Reversed* means that the lower court's opinion is found in error and any judgment or decision of the lower court based on that opinion is vacated, i.e., rendered void.

In **subsequent treatment**, the proposition from your case (the *cited* case) could have been overruled, distinguished or otherwise treated negatively in an unrelated, later case (a *citing* case). That too can change the status of the law set forth in the case. *Overruled* means that the legal reasoning in the cited case is disavowed and the cited case may no longer be cited as good law for the overruled proposition. *Distinguished* means that the cited case is held inapplicable due to a difference in law or fact.

Finally, there may have been a **non-judicial change in law**, such as legislation that effectively overturned a point of law in your case. Such a change may be noted in later court decisions.

In any of these situations, your case may no longer be authoritative on the point for which you would like to cite it; in other words, it may not be "good law" and should not be relied upon.

Lists of cases and other authority impacting your case are found in **citators**.

The first citator was published by Frank Shepard in 1875. Shepard initially published his citation lists in the form of "adhesive annotations" that were pasted directly to the first page of the case in print. The annotation listed other cases citing to and impacting the reported case. Eventually, Shepard would publish his citations in printed volumes specific to individual jurisdictions. Shepard's product was so successful that his name was turned into a verb, "to Shepardize," which describes the act of updating. Today, Shepard's is available in print and online through LexisNexis.

Frank Shepard (1848-1902)

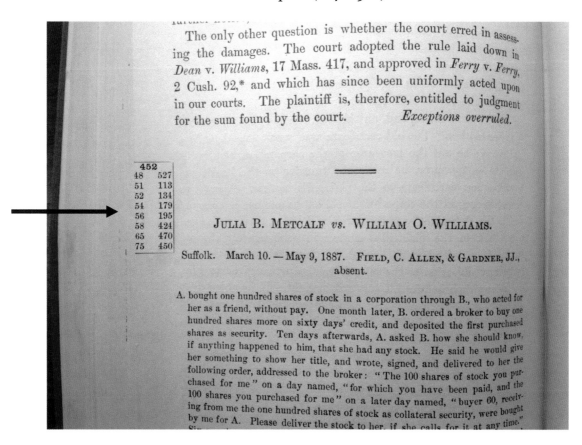

A page of the Massachusetts Reports from 1887 showing the adhesive annotations

Citators are used to locate cases that impact the case on which you are relying. Traditionally, researchers used *Shepard's Citations* in print volumes. For every reported case, *Shepard's* provided lists of citations to cases that cited to it, including citations to cases that treated the reported case negatively. A representative page from a modern version of *Shepard's* in print, showing citations to cases reported in volumes 438 and 439 of the Northeastern Reporter, 2d Series, is shown below.

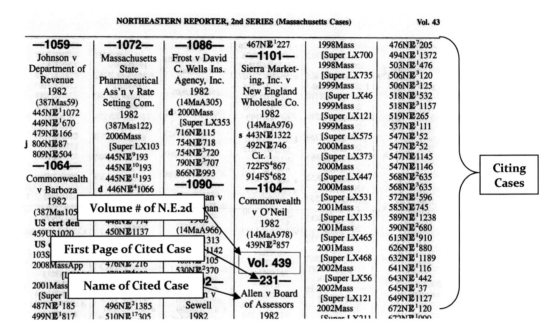

Below is an example of *Shepard's Citations* from 1902, showing citations to U.S. Supreme Court cases.

Though they still exist, *Shepard's* in print and other print citators are relics only. You should not use them if you have access to an online citator as the online citator will always be the most up-to-date citator available. (Can you explain why it is important to have the most up-to-date information available when updating?)

This chapter will discuss two online citators, **Shepard's** on Lexis Advance (the direct descendant of the original print *Shepard's*) and **KeyCite** on WestlawNext. (Please note: Some researchers may use other citators, such as BCite on Bloomberg Law, citators developed by other commercial database providers, or the citator in a topical service that focuses on, *e.g.,* tax or securities law.)

*   *   *

Shepard's and KeyCite

Shepard's and KeyCite are distinct products with their own formats and vocabularies, but they nevertheless have key features in common. Notably, both citators use visual symbols to indicate negative or positive treatment of a case; these symbols mimic traffic signals, with the colors (red and yellow, and sometimes green or blue) conveying the different levels of caution you should employ when citing a case.

The most negative treatment is assigned a red symbol (red flag on KeyCite, red stop sign on Shepard's). The red symbols provide strong indications that your case is no longer authoritative for at least one point of law and that you should "Stop" before relying on it. Likewise, the yellow symbols (yellow flag on KeyCite, yellow yield sign on Shepard's) convey that there is some negative treatment of your case and that you should slow down or exercise caution prior to citing it. And, finally, green (and sometimes blue) means that your case is still good law for all its points of law and that you can "Go" ahead and cite it without worry.

Please see the next page for a list of symbols or indicators for Shepard's and KeyCite.

Shepard's Symbols (case law)

Research Tip: Reading Shepard's Symbols

● **Warning-Negative treatment indicated**
The red Shepard's Signal indicates that citing references in the Shepard's® Citations Service contain strong negative history or treatment of your case (for example, overruled by or reversed).

▲ **Caution-Possible negative treatment indicated**
The yellow Shepard's Signal indicates that citing references in the Shepard's Citations Service contain history or treatment that may have a significant negative impact on your case (for example, limited or criticized by).

◆ **Positive treatment indicated**
The green Shepard's Signal indicates that citing references in the Shepard's Citations Service contain history or treatment that has a positive impact on your case (for example, affirmed or followed by).

Ⓐ **Cited and neutral analysis indicated**
The blue "A" Shepard's Signal indicates that citing references in the Shepard's Citations Service contain treatment of your case that is neither positive nor negative.

Ⓘ **Citation information available**
The blue "I" Shepard's Signal indicates that citing references are available in the Shepard's Citations Service for your case, but the references do not have history or treatment analysis (for example, the references are law review citations).

NOTE: Not every case will have a signal indicator.

KeyCite Symbols (case law)

▷ **Red Flag** - Your case is no longer good law for at least one of the points it contains.

▷ **Yellow Flag** - Your case has had some negative history but hasn't been reversed or overruled.

Ⓗ **Blue H** - Your case has some history.

Ⓒ **Green C** - Your case has citing references but no direct or negative indirect history.

The updating process does not end with these symbols. As noted above, the red and yellow symbols only communicate case treatment messages to the researcher in very broad terms. It is your responsibility to consult the various decisions themselves in both the *direct history* and other later *citing decisions*, and to read enough of those decisions to form a conclusion as to whether the case you're checking, the *cited* decision, is still "good law." From the lists of later decisions provided by an online citator, you can click on links to jump to the cases in the history or the citing decisions, and read them.

For an example, let's use a prominent (and very widely cited) case, the Supreme Court's landmark ruling that established a woman's constitutional right to have an abortion, *Roe v. Wade*, 410 U.S. 113 (1973). When viewing this case on Lexis Advance, the researcher likely notices a red stop sign symbol next to the case name.

⬤ **Roe v. Wade, 410 U.S. 113** (Copy citation)

Supreme Court of the United States
December 13, 1971, Argued ; January 22, 1973, Decided
No. 70-18

From the red stop sign, the researcher might infer that *Roe* is not good law, but that judgment would be premature. At times, a case may be rejected in part by the court that decided it, or by other courts, and still be useful in your analysis. Here, *Roe* is not merely one case on the topic, but the foundational case in this area of law, decided by the U.S. Supreme Court. If one were working on a project related to a woman's constitutional right to have an abortion, it would be necessary to form a conclusion about the current status of *Roe*. That would require checking later cases to find out what negative treatment resulted in the red symbol and what those cases mean for the continuing validity of *Roe*. Shepard's can identify which of those later cases are most significant, but it remains the researcher's job to read the cases before reaching a conclusion.

Shepardize®

The full Shepard's report on Roe can be accessed by clicking on either the red stop sign or the "Shepardize" button above the report of the case. The first screen displays the prior and subsequent direct history or **Appellate History** of the case. Above the Appellate History, Shepard's provides a note, "No subsequent negative appellate history." Thus, while the decisions listed in the direct history of *Roe* may be of interest, **the direct or appellate history does not explain why Shepard's editors assigned the red symbol**.

The next tab at the top of the Shepard's Report is for **Citing Decisions**. This tab indicates that (over a 40 year period) nearly 4,000 later cases have cited to *Roe v. Wade*. This very large number may seem overwhelming, but it is not necessary to consult more than a few of these decisions. First, when updating, we are mostly concerned with negative treatment by the same court or higher courts in the same jurisdiction. Because there is no higher federal court, we are almost exclusively concerned with negative treatment of *Roe* by subsequent decisions of the U.S. Supreme Court. After clicking the Citing Decisions tab for *Roe*, we go to a page that begins to list those decisions.

On the left side of the new page, there is a summary that lists cases arranged under various **Analysis** categories: from most to least negative treatment; then positive treatment; then "neutral" treatment; and finally those merely "cited by" decisions. Here, alongside the red stop sign and the word "Warning," there are two entries indicating that Roe has been "Overruled in part by" one of them, and for the other, "Overruled in part as stated in."

Narrow by...

⌄ Analysis

🔴 **Warning(2)**

Overruled in part by	1
Overruled in part ...	1

Questioned(6)

Questioned by	6

Caution(139)

Distinguished by	131
Criticized by	9

Positive(217)

Followed by	217

Neutral(498)

Cited in Dissentin...	258
Cited in Concurrin...	181
Explained by	81
Cited in questiona...	11
Criticized in Conc...	5
Harmonized by	4
Dissenting opinion...	1
Distinguished by q...	1
Distinguished in C...	1
Explained in Concu...	1
Explained by quest...	1

"Cited by"(3,417)

Clicking on "Warning" leads to information about *Planned Parenthood v. Casey* (1992) and *Gonzales v. Carhart* (2007); both are key abortion rights cases that a researcher would need to consult to determine the current status of *Roe*.

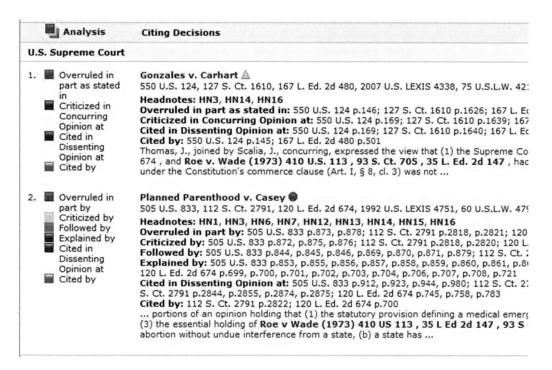

Below the Warning listing, there is a list of other negative treatment categories—Questioned by, Caution (including cases that *criticize Roe*)— and then Positive cases, Neutral cases and several thousand "Cited by" references. In reality, it would not be necessary to check more than a few cases from the negative treatment categories, but a researcher would need to read *Casey* and *Carhart* and check enough other cases to determine whether a particular point of law in *Roe* is still "good law" in light of the later decisions of the Supreme Court. A third Supreme Court case that provides negative treatment of *Roe* is *Webster v. Reproductive Health Services* (1989), which can be found among the cases that criticize Roe, under the category Caution.

*   *   *

Updating Roe v. Wade Using KeyCite

Now, compare the treatment of *Roe v. Wade* by Westlaw's citator, KeyCite. When viewing *Roe v. Wade* on WestlawNext, KeyCite information is visible at the top of the screen, above the case caption. There is a yellow flag next to the name of the case and there is a row of tabs above the case report labeled **Filings, History, Negative Treatment,** and **Citing References.** Negative Treatment and Citing References are the key tabs to use when updating.

In KeyCite, the yellow flag means that there is "some negative history" for a cited case. (By comparison, the red flag is a much stronger symbol, meaning that "a document is no longer good law for at least one point of law.")

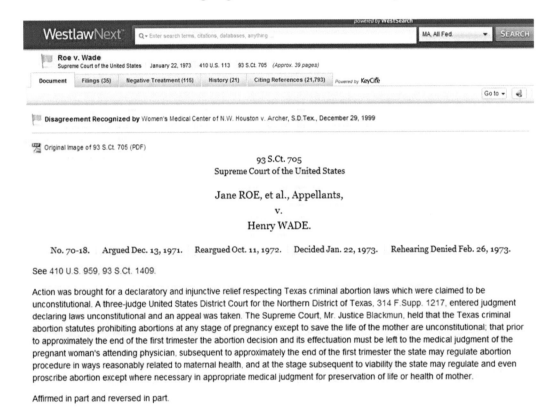

Often, the editors at KeyCite and Shepard's will assign the same color symbols to a case; but here, they did not. These differing characterizations by the editors on the status of such a major Supreme Court decision reinforce the point above; a researcher must form her own conclusion about the status of a case after checking the subsequent history and later citing references for a case.

If you click on the yellow flag, KeyCite jumps to the **Negative Treatment** tab. Here, there are two sections. Under the first, Negative Direct History, KeyCite (like Shepard's) tells us, "There is no negative direct history." The second section, Negative Treatment, includes a list of over 100 cases. As we saw with Shepard's, it is not necessary to consult more than a few of these cases. In the KeyCite display below, two cases stand out because they were decided by the Supreme Court and the treatment column indicates a significant impact on the status of the holding in *Roe*: "Holding Limited by" *Webster v. Reproductive Health Services* (1989) and "Holding Modified by" *Planned Parenthood v. Casey* (1992).

☐ Holding Limited by	⚑ 7. Webster v. Reproductive Health Services 〃	Jul. 03 , 1989
	492 U.S. 490, U.S.Mo.	
	State-employed health care professionals and facilities offering abortion counseling and services brought class action seeking declaration and injunctive relief challenging...	
☐ Holding Modified by	⚑ 8. Planned Parenthood of Southeastern Pennsylvania v. Casey 〃	Jun. 29 , 1992
	505 U.S. 833, U.S.Pa.	
	Abortion clinics and physician challenged, on due process grounds, the constitutionality of the 1988 and 1989 amendments to the Pennsylvania abortion statute. The United States...	

To determine the current status of *Roe*, it is necessary to read *Webster* and *Casey* and assess how those later decisions by the Supreme Court modified or limited the holding in *Roe*. Like Shepards, KeyCite provides links to jump to the full text of all citing decisions. Please note: the yellow flags placed next to these citing cases in the table refer to negative treatment **of those cases**, not of *Roe*.

KeyCite summarizes each case listed under Negative Treatment with phrases such as: "Called into Doubt by," "Disagreement Recognized by," "Declined to Extend by." Aside from *Webster* and *Casey*, nearly all the cases providing negative treatment of *Roe* are from *lower* federal courts and state courts. (The exception is *Gonzales v. Carhart* (2007), noted in the discussion of Shepard's above, a Supreme Court case near the end of the negative treatment list on KeyCite.)

As noted before, for updating purposes we are mostly concerned with cases decided by the Supreme Court that provide negative treatment of *Roe*. This does not mean that the lower court cases are worthless. For example, if we were especially concerned about the law regarding abortion rights in the Eighth Circuit, we may want to check *Coe v. Melahn*, an 8th Circuit case that, according to KeyCite, "called [*Roe*] into doubt," to see what it tells us about that Circuit's reading of *Roe*.

The KeyCite tab for **Citing References** lists well over 20,000 documents that cite *Roe v. Wade,* but the use of the filters on the left hand panel helps us to identify quickly the most important cases for updating purposes. (We can disregard secondary sources and other types of material.) To identify the key cases among this long list of citing references, under VIEW, click on "Cases."

VIEW	«
Cases	3,775
Administrative Decisions & Guidance	271
Secondary Sources	12,979
Appellate Court Documents	3,681
Trial Court Documents	1,087
All Results	21,793

Then, use additional filters to limit the results.

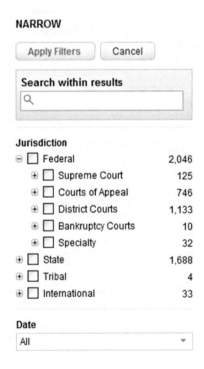

NARROW

Apply Filters   Cancel

Search within results

Jurisdiction

Federal	2,046
Supreme Court	125
Courts of Appeal	746
District Courts	1,133
Bankruptcy Courts	10
Specialty	32
State	1,688
Tribal	4
International	33

Date

All

Under "Jurisdiction," open the category "Federal"; then click the box next to Supreme Court. When you click the "Apply Filters" button, KeyCite displays the list of over 100 U.S. Supreme Court cases that have cited *Roe*. The most important cases appear at the top of the list: *Webster, Casey,* and *Gonzales v. Carhart*. For each case, the treatment information is embellished by a banner reading "Negative," the only three cases so designated. (The other Supreme Court cases are described as more positive or neutral toward *Roe*: "Examined by," "Discussed by," "Cited by.")

The depth of treatment bars (indicating one to four green boxes) in the *Depth* column indicate the extent to which the citing cases discuss the cited case, and the headnote numbers in the *Headnote(s)* column indicate which headnotes in the cited case contain the points of law discussed by the citing cases. The filters could be adjusted to find lower federal or state courts, including those commenting negatively on *Roe*, if we wanted to see them here.

Treatment	Title	Date	Type	Depth ▾
Holding Limited by NEGATIVE	1. Webster v. Reproductive Health Services 〃 109 S.Ct. 3040, 3042+, U.S.Mo. State-employed health care professionals and facilities offering abortion counseling and services brought class action seeking declaration and injunctive relief challenging...	Jul. 03, 1989	Case	▰▰▰▰
Holding Modified by NEGATIVE	2. Planned Parenthood of Southeastern Pennsylvania v. Casey 〃 112 S.Ct. 2791, 2796+, U.S.Pa. Abortion clinics and physician challenged, on due process grounds, the constitutionality of the 1988 and 1989 amendments to the Pennsylvania abortion statute. The United States...	Jun. 29, 1992	Case	▰▰▰▰
Modification Recognized by NEGATIVE	3. Gonzales v. Carhart 〃 127 S.Ct. 1610, 1614+, U.S. FAMILY LAW - Abortion. Ban on partial-birth abortion procedure was not void for vagueness or unconstitutional due to lack of health exception.	Apr. 18, 2007	Case	▰▰▰▰

To summarize, to determine if *Roe* is still good law, we could use either the Negative Treatment tab or the Citing References tab. Although the latter lists far more documents, it also provides for filtering the results, a quicker way to identify the three cases that matter most to us: Supreme Court cases that provide negative treatment of *Roe*. In this instance, the Citing References tab is a more efficient route to the key cases than scrolling through several screens of case references under the Negative Treatment tab. Like Shepard's, KeyCite suggests that some but not all part(s) of *Roe* have been limited or modified by later Supreme Court decisions. Once we have identified the key cases, we can read them and determine what they mean for the current status of *Roe*.

Updating Statutes

Both Shepard's and KeyCite can be used to check the status of other legal authorities, including statutes. For example, consider the treatment of the federal statute that prohibited flag desecration, 18 U.S.C. § 700. Both Shepard's and KeyCite provide information that can quickly inform us of significant negative treatment of the statute in the case law.

In Shepard's, there are two visual symbols that indicate updating information is available for a statute. A red exclamation point symbol indicates negative treatment.

By clicking the link alongside the exclamation point that reads "View Shepard's Report," we go directly to a **Citing Decisions** tab. In the **Analysis** sidebar to the left, citing decisions are grouped into several categories, including **Warning**. Below Warning we see that there are three cases that have declared this statute unconstitutional.

Narrow by...	
⊻ **Analysis**	
ⓘ **Warning(3)**	
Unconstitutional by	3
Positive(5)	
Constitutional by	5
"Cited by"(54)	
	Select Multiple
⊻ **Court**	
Federal Courts(39)	
U.S. Supreme Court	7
11th Circuit	5
D.C. Circuit	5
9th Circuit	4
1st Circuit	3
More	Select Multiple
State Courts(22)	
Ohio	4
Texas	3
California	2
Dist. of Columbia	2
Pennsylvania	2
More	Select Multiple

Clicking on "Warning" retrieves the three cases so holding, including *United States v. Eichman*, a Supreme Court decision.

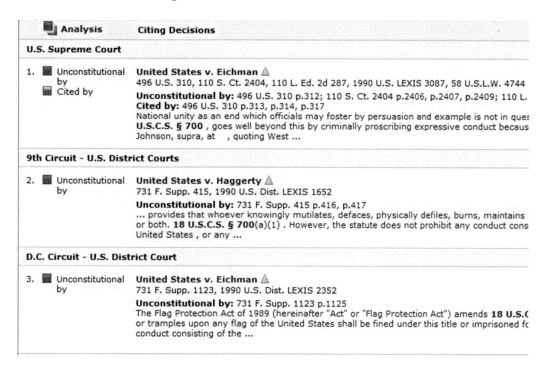

As when updating cases, a researcher must read the most significant citing decisions for herself and form her own conclusion. Given the invalidating decision by the Supreme Court, it appears very likely that this section of the U.S. Code is no longer in force. Had only a lower federal court declared the section to be invalid, however, that court's decision would have had force only in one circuit or district.

Checking the same section on Westlaw Next, KeyCite information appears directly above section 700.

18 U.S.C.A. § 700

§ 700. Desecration of the flag of the United States; penalties

There is a red flag and the notation, "Unconstitutional or Preempted: Held Unconstitutional by," with a link to the Supreme Court's *Eichman* decision. For fuller information, we can consult the KeyCite information tabs near the top of the screen or click the red flag, which takes us to the History tab.

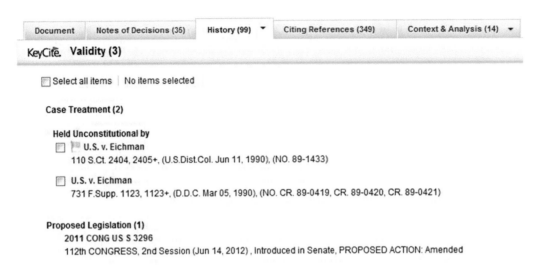

As of early 2013, the History tab shows two cases holding section 700 unconstitutional and a bill in the 112th Congress that would have amended the section, if it had passed. These same authorities can be found by clicking to see materials on the section's "Validity" under the History tab. The Citing References tab provides links to many more cases and other citing references, in a format similar to the KeyCite display for updating cases.

With both Lexis Advance and Westlaw Next, the cases invalidating section 700 also could be found using the case annotations in the annotated codes (*United States Code Annotated* (U.S.C.A.) in Westlaw Next; *United States Code Service* (U.S.C.S.) in Lexis Advance). But the citators highlight the cases that provide negative treatment of the section and provide us also with links to any pending legislation that (if passed into law) would amend the section we are updating, which the annotated codes do not.

In Westlaw Next, the Notes of Decisions tab provides us with case annotations from the U.S.C.A., seamlessly integrated with KeyCite and listed on a separate tab. In Lexis Advance, the Shepard's treatment of the statutory section is separated from the U.S.C.S. materials, but it requires only a click to move from section 700 to the Shepard's report.

Even if section 700 had not been declared unconstitutional in the courts, the yellow symbols (a flag on KeyCite, a triangle in Shepard's) would signal any pending legislation. However, the pending legislation notations should not be taken to suggest a section of the United States Code is not currently in force. Thousands of bills are introduced in Congress every year; the vast majority of them do not become law. The yellow signal provides the researcher with a quick way to locate the text of the bills, and then to check on the bills' status. In some situations, this may be valuable updating information for a researcher.

The Shepard's and KeyCite symbols for statutes are below.

Shepard's

Ⓘ   *Warning: Negative treatment is indicated for statute*

△   *Caution: Possible negative treatment indicated*

◆   *Positive treatment indicated*

KeyCite

A red flag indicates that the statute has been

Recently amended
Repealed
Ruled unconstitutional
Preempted

A yellow flag indicates that the statute

- Has pending legislation
- Has been renumbered
- Has been transferred
- Contains an editor's amendment note
- Was limited on constitutional or preemption grounds or its validity was otherwise called into doubt

Using Shepard's and KeyCite for Research

Shepard's and KeyCite were developed primarily to allow attorneys to update their research. Over time, however, the availability of so much information about the treatment of cases has permitted a secondary purpose—the expansion of research.

To use an example, your client entered into a covenant not to compete clause as part of his employment agreement. He is a hair dresser and the covenant not to compete specified that he could not work as a hair dresser within a 50 mile radius of his former employer for five years. You want to find out if this clause is enforceable in Massachusetts. You find a leading case after going to Massachusetts Practice and looking at the volumes on Employment Law, *Marine Contractors Co., Inc. v. Hurley*, 365 Mass. 280, 284, 310 N.E.2d 915, 918 (1974). This is a Supreme Judicial Court case from 1974, so first you need to update the case. There is no negative treatment of this case, so it is good law. But have courts expanded on the concepts articulated in this case?

This is an important question. And, by recalling that Shepard's and KeyCite also provide **positive** citing references, you can readily answer it.

You can use Shepard's or KeyCite to find other cases that talk about this area of law and other important cases or concepts. From *Hurley's* KeyCite display, you can limit the citing references by jurisdiction, as discussed above, to Massachusetts state cases. Then you can limit the headnotes to cases that cite this important case and discuss the concept of "Limitations as to Time and Place in General" and "Extent of Territory Embraced in General" with regard to covenants not to compete.

The result?

Thirty-two cases that you know, prior to even reading them, discuss concepts regarding the enforceability of covenents not to compete that are important to your case and that also cite to the leading case in this area.

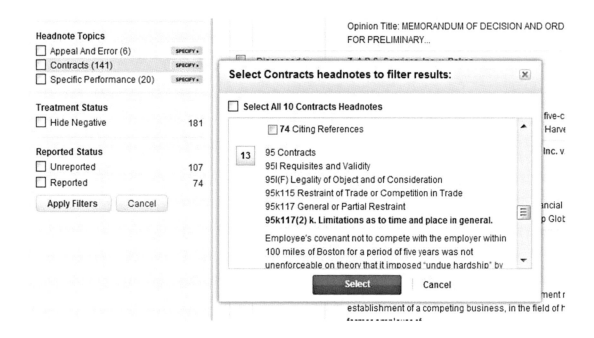

On Shepard's the headnotes are not as well developed. You can use headnotes as well to sort your results, but there is another way to filter your results that is quite effective. You can search within your results—this means you are searching only those cases that cited your leading case. By searching for "miles or distance" within your Shepard's results, you narrow your search to the 37 decisions that discuss the concept of distance. When you view your results you are able to focus on that part of each decision that mentions your keywords. This is another effective way of limiting your results to cases that cite the leading case and are relevant to your fact pattern.

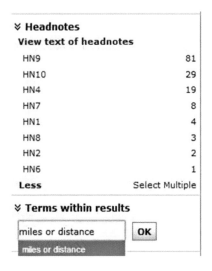

In this example you have used Shepard's and Keycite as research tools, both updating your case and finding other cases that might be relevant to your research.

*   *   *

Practice Questions

Use KeyCite in Westlaw Next for these questions

1. Why did KeyCite identify *Lawrence v. Texas* as the "Most Negative" case that cited *Bowers v. Hardwick*, 478 U.S. 186 (1986)?

2. Is there any negative treatment of *Lawrence* by later U.S. Supreme Court decisions?

3. Consult KeyCite re *Catholic Charities of Sacramento v. Superior Court*, 32 Cal.4th 527 (Cal. 2004). Does it appear that this case still good law? Explain.

4. Consult the History tab for the Direct History of *Catholic Charities*. Is the action taken by the U.S. Supreme Court support your previous answer?

5. Re *Greenslade v. Mohawk Park, Inc.*, 798 N.E.2d 336 (Mass App. Ct. 2003), how does information in KeyCite about the "most negative" case explain KeyCite's assignment of a yellow flag?

6. Consult the passage in that most negative case where *Greenslade* was discussed. According to the court, how were the facts in that case different from those in *Greenslade*?

7. Name five of the states whose courts have rejected, disagreed with or declined to follow the landmark ruling by the Massachusetts' Supreme Judicial Court in *Goodridge v. Department of Public Health*, 440 Mass. 309 (2003).

8. The so-called health insurance "mandate" provision in the Patient Protection and Affordable Care Act, 26 U.S.C.A. 5000A, was held unconstitutional by some federal courts. Consult the information that displays above section 5000A on Westlaw Next. Why did KeyCite <u>not</u> assign a red flag to this provision?

9. Consult the Citing References for §5000A. Are any American Law Reports (ALR) annotations cited?

10. Again, start with the Citing References tab. Use the filters in the column to the left side of the screen to locate cases decided by the U.S. Courts of Appeals that cite section 5000A. In the resulting list, what visual symbol does KeyCite place alongside several of the cases that were decided in 2011? What does that symbol mean?

Use Shepard's on Lexis Advance for these Questions

11. Consult *Austin v. Mich. State Chamber of Commerce*, 494 U.S. 652 (1990) on Lexis Advance. What visual symbol does Shepards Citations assign to the *Austin* case, and what language appears when you pass the cursor over that symbol?

12. Shepardize *Austin*. Consult the Appellate History tab. Does anything in the subsequent history of the case that indicates why this symbol was assigned to the Supreme Court's decision in Austin?

13. Next, consult the Citing Decisions tab and note the analysis menu to the left of the resulting page. Among the cases listed for providing negative treatment of *Austin*, what case is most significant? Why?

14. Does the Shepard's report on *Austin* indicate positive treatment also?

15. Consult *Goodridge v. Department of Public Health*, 440 Mass. 309 (2003) on Lexis Advance. What symbol does Shepard's Citations assign to this case, and what language appears when you point the cursor at that symbol?

16. Consult the Citing Decisions tab. Are any of the cases listed as providing negative treatment of *Goodridge* from Massachusetts state courts?

17. According to the Shepard's Citations information, does it appear that *Goodridge* still good law?

18. Does the Shepard's report for *Goodridge* indicate any citing decisions from Alaska state courts? If so, provide the citation(s) to the first or oldest one.

19. Click on the link to go to that Alaska case, and note the citation to *Goodridge* in this case. Where does the citation appear and how is it called to your attention?

20. Shepardize the Alaska case. What symbol does Shepard's assign to it, and why?

Notes

Notes

Answer Key for Updating Practice Questions

Use KeyCite in Westlaw Next for these Questions

1. Why did KeyCite identify *Lawrence v. Texas* as the "Most Negative" case that cited *Bowers v. Hardwick*, 478 U.S. 186 (1986)?

   Because *Lawrence* overruled *Bowers*

2. Is there any negative treatment of *Lawrence* by later U.S. Supreme Court decisions?

   No. (Under Citing Reference, using filters to limit the display to U.S. Supreme Court decisions, all the 15 or more cases have positive or neutral references to *Lawrence*—e.g., "Cited by," "Examined by," or "Mentioned by.")

3. Consult KeyCite re *Catholic Charities of Sacramento v. Superior Court*, 32 Cal.4th 527 (Cal. 2004). Does it appear that this case still good law? Explain.

   Yes. No cases are listed as providing negative treatment of this case; thus, Key Cite has not assigned a red or yellow flag to it.

4. Consult the History tab for the Direct History of *Catholic Charities*. Is the action taken by the U.S. Supreme Court support your previous answer?

   Yes. By denying *certiorari*, the Supreme Court left the California Supreme Court's decision intact.

5. Re *Greenslade v. Mohawk Park, Inc.*, 798 N.E.2d 336 (Mass App. Ct. 2003), how does information in KeyCite about the "most negative" case explain KeyCite's assignment of a yellow flag?

   In the "most negative" case, *Greenslade* was "distinguished by" *Godsoe v. Maple Park Properties, Inc.* There is no indication that *Greenslade* has been overturned. The yellow flag indicates there is some negative history.

6. Consult the passage in that most negative case where *Greenslade* was discussed. According to the court, how were the facts in that case different from those in *Greenslade*?

   In *Greenslade*, the question of an "open and obvious danger" involved "the activity of rope-swinging over a rock-strewn river"; in *Godsoe*, the injured minor was using a slide installed by defendant in a man-made lake.

7. Name five of the states whose courts have rejected, disagreed with or declined to follow the landmark ruling by the Massachusetts' Supreme Judicial Court in *Goodridge v. Department of Public Health*, 440 Mass. 309 (2003).

   Washington, New York, New Jersey, California, Connecticut and Indiana
   Check the cases listed on the Negative Treatment tab; or under Citing References, consult the list of cases: those listed first have a "Negative" label attached to them.

8. The so-called health insurance "mandate" provision in the Patient Protection and Affordable Care Act, 26 U.S.C.A. 5000A, was held unconstitutional by some federal courts. Consult the information that displays above section 5000A on Westlaw Next. Why did KeyCite <u>not</u> assign a red flag to this provision?

   Because the Supreme Court "reconsidered" those rulings and upheld the mandate provision in *National Federation of Independent Business v. Sebelius* (2012).

9. Consult the Citing References for §5000A. Are any American Law Reports (ALR) annotations cited?

   Yes, under Secondary Sources, at least three ALRs are included among the listed citations.

10. Again, start with the Citing References tab. Use the filters in the column to the left side of the screen to locate cases decided by the U.S. Courts of Appeals that cite section 5000A. In the resulting list, what visual symbol does KeyCite place alongside several of the cases that were decided in 2011? What does that symbol mean?

A red flag that refers to the status of those cases (not the status of section 5000A). According to KeyCite: "A red flag indicates a document is no longer good law for at least one point of law."

Use Lexis Advance for these Questions

11. Consult *Austin v. Mich. State Chamber of Commerce*, 494 U.S. 652 (1990) on Lexis Advance. What visual symbol does Shepard's Citations assign to the *Austin* case, and what language appears when you pass the cursor over that symbol?

    Red stop sign; "Warning: Negative Treatment is Indicated."

12. Shepardize Austin. Consult the Appellate History tab. Does anything in the subsequent history of the case that indicates why this symbol was assigned to the Supreme Court's decision in Austin?

    No. The only subsequent history was that this case was remanded to the Court of Appeals. There is no negative subsequent history.

13. Next, consult the Citing Decisions tab and note the analysis menu to the left of the resulting page. Among the cases listed for providing negative treatment of *Austin*, what case is most significant? Why?

    ***Citizens United v. FEC*. Because *Austin* was "overruled by" *Citizens United*.**

14. Does the Shepard's report on *Austin* indicate positive treatment also?

    Yes. Many cases are listed as following *Austin*.

15. Consult *Goodridge v. Department of Public Health*, 440 Mass. 309 (2003) on Lexis Advance. What symbol does Shepards Citations assign to this case, and what language appears when you point the cursor at that symbol?

Yellow triangle: "Caution: Possible negative treatment"

16. Consult the Citing Decisions tab. Are any of the cases listed as providing negative treatment of *Goodridge* from Massachusetts state courts?

   No. All are from other states.

17. According to the Shepard's Citations information, does it appear that *Goodridge* still good law?

   Yes. See previous question and answer.

18. Does the Shepard's report for *Goodridge* indicate any citing decisions from Alaska state courts? If so, provide the citation(s) to the first or oldest one.

   Yes, *Goodridge* was cited by *Alaska Civil Liberties Union v. State*, 122 P.3d 781 (2005).
   (Use the filters in the column to the left, and select Alaska among the state court jurisdictions.)

19. Click on the link to go to that Alaska case, and note the citation to *Goodridge* in this case. Where does the citation appear and how is it called to your attention?

   In footnote 66. The citation to *Goodridge* is highlighted in yellow.

20. Shepardize the Alaska case. What symbol does Shepard's assign to it, and why?

   Shepards assigned a yellow triangle because three cases (none of them from Alaska courts) "distinguished" the case.
   (Under Analysis in the left-hand column, the yellow triangle is placed next to "Caution"; under that, the entry is for "Distinguished by.")

Alternatives to High Cost Databases

Alternatives to High Cost Databases

Some No-Cost Alternatives for Legal Research

Legal research need not be expensive. Most primary and much secondary authority can be found for no cost at all. Indeed, we recommend that all law students develop a familiarity with at least a few free resources. Your future employers will most certainly appreciate it.

Some of our favorite options for no-cost legal research are below.

Congress.Gov

Link: http://beta.congress.gov

Congress.Gov provides extensive legislative information. Users can view the legislative history of passed laws and pending bills, including bill text, bill sponsors, committee action, and related bills. Timelines accompany each bill, so that users can easily tell how far the bill has made it in the legislative process—whether it has passed the House or Senate and been presented to the President. The site provides easy access to the Congressional Record, complete with the daily digest and floor remarks. Congress.Gov is also a good educational tool, and there are videos and literature explaining the legislative process.

Cornell LII

Link: http://www.law.cornell.edu

The Legal Information Institute is a comprehensive legal site. Users can access the U.S. Code, the C.F.R., federal rules, state statues, uniform laws, international law materials, and Supreme Court case law. The site also provides a legal dictionary and a legal encyclopedia, as well as a "find a lawyer" service.

Court Websites

Supreme Court: http://www.supremecourt.gov
Federal Courts: http://www.uscourts.gov/FederalCourts.aspx
First Circuit: http://www.ca1.uscourts.gov
District of Massachusetts: http://www.mad.uscourts.gov
Mass. State Courts: SJC: http://www.mass.gov/courts/sjc/

Court websites are a great place to find judicial opinions, briefs, and court records. Users can access rules and procedures applicable to a specific court, as well as attorney admission information. Perhaps most importantly, court websites provide users with nuts and bolts materials and information necessary for practice, including proper forms, guidelines, and fees.

Agency Websites

Securities and Exchange Commission: http://www.sec.gov
Federal Trade Commission: http://www.ftc.gov
The Fed: http://www.federalreserve.gov
Census Bureau: http://www.census.gov
The Congressional Budget Office: http://www.cbo.gov

Agency websites are the first place to search for agency rules and regulations, including orders from administrative law judges. They also house forms and public filings. Agency websites can provide information-rich government reports and statistics, as well as reviews on pending legislation. Agencies are also a great resource for cutting edge information regarding a specific issue area. For example, the SEC issues updates on litigation and regulatory orders that are vital to practitioners.

Google Scholar

Link: http://scholar.google.com

Google Scholar is a search engine that allows users to search for academic articles, books, and legal documents on a wide range of topics. It should be noted that many articles will be linked to commercial sites, thus allowing users to view only abstracts. However, students will often be granted the option to view the work via a school link, granting easier, free access. Searches can be sorted by relevance or date. Google Scholar can also be used to search court documents and cases with search terms, case names, or citations, and users can confine their searches to specific jurisdictions.

Thomas

Link: http://thomas.loc.gov/home/thomas.php

Thomas is the first place to start research on legislative history, as the Library of Congress provides extensive and easy access to legislative materials through the site. Users can search for bills and laws with keywords or bill numbers, can browse bills by sponsor, and can narrow searches by congressional committee or stage in the legislative process. Thomas is especially good for tracking bills over time by allowing users to expand searches over multiple Congresses. In addition to bills, Thomas also grants access to committee reports, treaties, and the congressional record.

GPO FDsys

Link: http://www.gpo.gov/fdsys/

The Government Printing Office's Federal Digital System stores government documents and information. The site features certain collections, such as the United States Code, Code of Federal Regulations, Congressional Bills, and government budgets. Users can easily browse government publications by collection, congressional committee, date, or government author. Users can also do a keyword search or retrieve documents by citation.

Books

Links: http://www.bu.edu/lawlibrary/, http://books.google.com

Really! Books serve as great secondary sources, and provide good starting points for research. Some books can be viewed online through Google Books or as an e-book. And, of course, books are also available in print!

SSRN, The Social Science Research Center

Link: http://www.ssrn.com

SSRN grants access to scholarly articles. Users can browse a wide range of topics dealing with the social sciences and humanities, including the law and economics. Keyword searches list results based on the number of pervious downloads, giving users a good idea of what articles have been the most viewed or cited. While not all articles are available for free download, most are and can be viewed in PDF format.

*   *   *

Some Low-Cost Alternatives for Legal Research

Just as students should be familiar with no-cost options for legal research, so too should they be familiar with lower cost options as well. Lower cost than what? Lower cost than Westlaw and Lexis.

Some of our favorite lower cost options are below.

HeinOnline

Link: http://home.heinonline.org

HeinOnline is the go-to place for searching law reviews as it has full runs for almost any law review you can name. As a bonus, all materials are presented in PDF format. Users can conduct keyword searches, and upon request HeinOnline will sort articles by the number of times cited. This gives users a sense of which articles have been most heavily relied upon by other scholars. Among many others, Hein Online also contains libraries for the U.S. Supreme Court, the U.S. Code, the C.F.R, the Federal Register, and Federal Legislative Histories.

LoisLaw

Link: http://estore.loislaw.com

Like Lexis and Westlaw, LoisLaw allows users to conduct keyword searches for primary legal materials, including state and federal cases, statutes, administrative regulations, and court rules. Users can also search secondary sources and treatises on certain practice areas.

Fastcase

Link: http://www.fastcase.com

Users can search cases, statutes, regulations, and court rules. Fastcase informs users how often a particular case has been cited, and provides excerpts from other relevant cases. Fastcase will also identify additional decisions that may be relevant to the user's research topic, but that do not contain one or more of the search terms.

Casemaker X

Link: http://www.casemakerx.com

Users can access federal and state statutes, cases, and regulations, selected bar association materials, and selected administrative agency materials. Newly added is Casecheck+, which uses icons to identify current case status with a link to the cited case in the citing case. Casemaker X also provides Casemaker Digest, which provides summaries of recent decisions published by the courts, within days of their publication.

Bloomberg Law

Link: http://about.bloomberglaw.com

Similar to Lexis and Westlaw, users can search cases, statutes, regulations, court filings, books, treatises, and law reviews. Bloomberg provides easy access to information regarding particular topics, specifically business and transactional law.

ProQuest Congressional

Link: http://congressional.proquest.com/congressional

This is a great place to search legislative history, in particular historical legislative history from the early 19th century to around 1990. Users can search bills, laws, the Congressional daily record, House and Senate documents and reports, CRS (Congressional Research Service) reports, and hearing transcripts. Users can also search by bill or public law number.

*   *   *

Notes

Notes

Made in the USA
Lexington, KY
21 August 2013